Women in the Global Economy:

Leading Social Change

Previous Titles in the Global Education Research Reports Series

U.S.-China Educational Exchange: Perspectives on a Growing Partnership

Higher Education on the Move: New Developments in Global Mobility

International India: A Turning Point in Educational Exchange with the U.S.

Innovation through Education: Building the Knowledge Economy in the Middle East

Who Goes Where and Why?: An Overview and Analysis of Global Educational Mobility

Developing Strategic International Partnerships: Models for Initiating and Sustaining Innovative Institutional Linkages

Latin America's New Knowledge Economy: Higher Education, Government, and International Collaboration

Women in the Global Economy:

Leading Social Change

EDITED BY TRISH TIERNEY

Eighth in a Series of Global Education Research Reports

New York

IIE publications can be purchased at: www.iiebooks.org

The Institute of International Education
809 United Nations Plaza, New York, New York 10017

Printed in the United States of America
ISBN 978-0-87206-359-4

Library of Congress Cataloging-in-Publication Data

Women in the global economy : leading social change / edited by Trish Tierney.
pages cm. -- (Global education research reports ; 8)
ISBN 978-0-87206-359-4 (pbk.)
1. Women in development. 2. Social change. 3. Women--Economic conditions. 4. Women--Social conditions. I. Tierney, Trish.
HQ1240.W6617 2013
305.42--dc23
2013004176

The views expressed in these chapters are solely those of the authors.
They do not necessarily represent the official positions of the
Institute of International Education or the AIFS Foundation.

Series Editors:
Daniel Obst, Deputy Vice President for International Partnerships, IIE
Sharon Witherell, Director of Public Affairs, IIE

Managing Editors: Daniel Obst, Madeline Friedman
Copy Editor: Teresa Barensfeld

Cover and text design: Pat Scully Design

Table of Contents

Figures and Tables

Figures

Forewords

BY ALLAN E. GOODMAN

An Arab proverb tells us, when you educate a woman, you create a nation. Today, leaders in every field must embrace gender equity as critical to thriving communities in our increasingly globalized world. Women are playing a significant and growing role in the economy. The last decade has been marked by great leaps for women here in the U.S. and around the globe, especially with the emergence of new technology and platforms that have given women greater voice.

But institutional and other obstacles remain and much more needs to be done.

At the Institute of International Education, we have made a commitment to furthering education and leadership opportunities for women and girls. IIE's Center for Women's Leadership Initiatives (WLI) provides for women worldwide to participate in cutting-edge training, professional development and exchange programs and to pursue higher education.

Through our programs, women develop and join networks of peers, mentors and experts and serve as effective leaders in the public and private sectors around the world. We work with sponsors to design programs that leverage strategic partnerships to engage emerging and established women leaders from underserved communities.

The very talented mentors from the San Francisco Bay Area and emerging leaders from the Middle East and North Africa who connect through TechWomen, an initiative of the U.S. Department of State's Bureau of Educational and Cultural Affairs, have demonstrated the incredible potential of such networks. In sub-Saharan Africa, strengthened centers of excellence in women's advocacy and leadership training, as well as courses in entrepreneurship and social media, have shown tremendous impact. We have learned from outstanding individuals and organizations in the course of this work, and have seen the power of supporting and partnering with new and established women leaders.

With this latest publication, we aim to share best practices from the field with corporate leaders, policy makers, philanthropists, intellectuals and educators. We hope this book will encourage them to enact and implement effective policies and programs to further enhance women's participation in the economic as well as the social sphere.

Allan E. Goodman

President & CEO, Institute of International Education

By William L. Gertz

AIFS is once again pleased to be collaborating with the Institute of International Education on the latest edition of the Global Education Research Reports.

This publication, "Women in the Global Economy: Leading Social Change" couldn't be more timely. The new U.S. Congress includes a record number of women; 101 across both chambers counting three non-voting members. Melanne Verveer was appointed as the Ambassador-at-Large for Global Women's Issues by President Obama after his administration created the position in 2009 (See her introduction to this publication). Secretary Clinton has made women's issues a major State Department priority and has created a number of innovative programs designed to bring more women to the U.S. to participate in cultural programs.

Those of us working in cultural exchange and international education have always been acutely aware of the role of women in our global society. As demographics continue to shift, more women are involved in our global economy and in leadership positions in international fields. Professionals working in our field are also primarily women, which can be traced back to the fact that many are study abroad alumni. At AIFS, four out of seven of our program directors are women.

Since our founding in 1964, AIFS has helped to provide opportunities for women to gain firsthand international experience through our cultural exchange and educational programs. Our participants have achieved a greater understanding of the world, vital language skills and the ability to function in different cultures.

Nearly 300,000 young women from more than 120 nations have experienced life in the United States through AIFS as au pairs, high school exchange students, camp counselors or as participants in our various summer programs. Many have returned to their native country with firsthand experience of other nations, cultures and greater global awareness. Cultural exchange participants were among the first visitors to America when the Soviet Union fell, enabling Eastern Europeans to travel abroad for the first time. Au pairs were among the first U.S. visitors after Apartheid ended and the South African travel ban was lifted. Even today, women from the nations of the Arab Spring are currently participating on our programs.

AIFS has sent more than half a million U.S. women abroad on study abroad and travel programs. These experiences are often their very first international experience and this alone is significant. For example, American women studying abroad were present when the Berlin Wall fell and were among the first to visit the former Soviet Union and China.

We are very proud to have played a small role in providing opportunities for women to become a force for social change, equality and global economic development. We are pleased to sponsor this important publication and are indebted to IIE and the authors for their scholarship.

William L. Gertz

President and Chief Executive Officer, American Institute For Foreign Study (AIFS)
Trustee, AIFS Foundation

Editor's Note

In September 2011, I had the good fortune to participate in the first-ever Asia Pacific Economic Cooperation (APEC) Women and the Economy Summit. This historical event was driven by the leadership of former Secretary of State Hillary Rodham Clinton, and like so many initiatives launched during her time in office, it was designed not only to inspire, but to spur action for change. As I listened to Secretary Clinton and other incredible speakers—women who had achieved the highest levels of success and impact in business, government and civil society, the idea for this volume was born.

That day, Secretary Clinton said: "Some leaders are born women." Her words ring true now more than ever, around the world, and in a host of fields. Women leaders drive change through political movements, emerging market growth, or grassroots activism. Yet, too often, their stories are not told.

This book reviews an inspiring transformation, one that in recent years has grown from a spark of ideas to lights gleaming around the world: the collective recognition that investing in women is not only necessary and effective, but that it delivers the kind of high-impact social and economic returns that are critical to the global economy, and to society as a whole.

Through IIE's Center for Women's Leadership Initiatives, the Institute places significant focus on supporting and partnering with emerging and established women leaders. We are pleased to offer a publication that recognizes women's impact around the world. We look forward to reading about the many success stories of tomorrow that may be inspired by the stories we chronicle here.

This book was made possible by all the women leaders included in these pages, and with the generous support from the AIFS Foundation. They have my deepest gratitude. I would also like to thank my colleagues, Lina Al-Eryani, Luke Eppelin, Patty Esposito, Madeline Friedman, Mary Karam McKey, Daniel Obst and Nicole Wood for their important contributions.

Trish Tierney

Introduction

WOMEN IN THE GLOBAL ECONOMY: LEADING SOCIAL CHANGE

MELANNE VERVEER, FORMER U.S. AMBASSADOR-AT-LARGE FOR GLOBAL WOMEN'S ISSUES

A plethora of studies over the past few years have shown that "gender equality is smart economics," a term properly coined by the World Bank. The untapped potential of women remains a lost opportunity for economic growth and development that the world can ill afford. Women's economic participation promotes poverty alleviation, agricultural productivity, enterprise development at both the micro and small and medium enterprise (SME) levels, as well as enhancing business management and returns on investment.

Investing in women produces a multiplier effect—women reinvest a large portion of their income in their families and communities. Women also play key roles in creating peaceful and stable societies—important factors for economic growth. Unfortunately, these benefits have not been universally recognized and have therefore not translated into women's full economic participation. Women still face obstacles when trying to establish new businesses or expand existing ones. Among the biggest hurdles are discriminatory laws, regulations and business conditions, as well as women's lack of access to property rights, as well as capital, training, technology, markets, mentors, and networks.

The Institute of International Education's publication, *Women in the Global Economy: Leading Social Change*, includes a wide range of issues concerning women in the economy. From farmers, informal sector workers, entrepreneurs, and business leaders, to social entrepreneurs, the book attempts to discuss the significant roles and contributions women play and give to the global economy. In addition, the book explores new tools such as technology, social media, and market-based approaches in enabling women's equal participation.

Jeni Klugman and Sarah Twigg from the World Bank give a comprehensive overview of the state of women, development, and gender equality. They argue that the dearth of gender disaggregated data is limiting effective and impactful investments in women, and that existing quantitative research misses gender dimensions of poverty such as time use and agency. In line with the same argument, Harvard professor Martha Chen examines the large share of women in informal employment and the diverse economic activities they engage in—trade, self-employment, entrepreneurship, and high-end goods and services production. Chen sees the working poor, especially women, as part of a global solution to increase growth and to decrease poverty and inequality.

In order to enable women to be full participants in the economy, Mary Ellen Iskenderian from Women's World Banking delves into women's access to capital and microfinance, calling for more attention to women's needs which go beyond credit. "Microfinance has been effective in some markets because of its ability to reach clients." "There is, however, much more to full financial inclusion," says Iskenderian. Savings, insurances, and other innovative financial products that serve women's needs can help incorporate women into the formal financial system which is good for economies, businesses, families and communities. Mobile banking, for example, has been identified as an effective tool to give women greater control over their financial futures by giving them direct financial services.

While the global gender gap in information and communications technologies (ICT) remains huge, Ann Mei Chang from the U.S. Department of State believes that the world should capture the opportunity to harness women's potential in unlocking the transformative benefits ICT can bring to development. Beth Kanter, a social media expert, further argues that women are networking experts, and transferring their skills to online social networking platforms can potentially help women achieve economic independence and sustainability.

While every author argues for a tool for women's economic empowerment, everyone agrees that partnerships are key to success. Penny Abeywardena from the Clinton Global Initiative introduces the "market-based approach"—forging public and private partnerships to grow women's opportunities through market expansion. Those market-based innovations often come from social entrepreneurs who solve social problems through pattern-breaking change, as Nuket Kardam and Fredric

Kropp elaborate in their article. And women social entrepreneurs are spearheading social change at local, national, and global levels, including women during the Arab Spring. The images of women fighting for freedom and democracy, as well as their own equality as portrayed by Arwa Othman, epitomized the new pages of women's movement throughout the region.

The case of women's contribution to the global economy and society has been made with evidence, but we need much more knowledge on best practices to further our investments in women and girls. This book is a collection of ideas that have been tested and proven. I hope there will be many more to come to enrich our understanding and resources for women's economic empowerment.

Melanne Verveer
Former U.S. Ambassador-at-Large for Global Women's Issues

Chapter One

Gender in Development: Investing in Women and Girls

Jeni Klugman, Gender and Development Unit, World Bank

Sarah Twigg, Gender and Development Unit, World Bank

Investing in Women and Girls Is the Right Thing to Do; It's the Smart Thing to Do

It is now widely recognized that gender equality is a core development objective in its own right. The World Development Report 2012: *Gender Equality and Development* (hereinafter, WDR 2012; World Bank, 2012a) emphasized that the enjoyment of equal rights and opportunities by women and men has intrinsic value for women's individual well-being and quality of life. This is in line with Amartya Sen's view of development, that it is the process of enlarging a person's "functionings and capabilities to function, the range of things that a person could do and be in her life" (Sen, 1989).

The views expressed in this chapter are solely those of the authors and do not reflect those of the World Bank or its executive directors.

But investing in women is also the smart thing to do. The WDR 2012 shows that investing in women can enhance productivity, improve development outcomes for the next generation, and make institutions more representative. Women's participation in state, social, and economic institutions helps to introduce new ideas and innovation into the economy and supports the development process. The United Nations has recognized these developmental benefits, acknowledging that gender equality is in fact a "prerequisite" to achieving the other Millennium Development Goals (United Nations, 2005, p. 14).

Gender equality is multidimensional. The WDR 2012 defines the key dimensions as threefold: endowments, opportunities, and agency. This encompasses the accumulation of endowments (education, health, and physical assets), the use of those endowments to take up economic opportunities and generate incomes, and the ability to make effective choices and transform those choices into desired outcomes (World Bank, 2012a). This chapter touches on each of these dimensions. We begin by providing an overview of recent trends and patterns in expanding women's endowments, opportunities, and agency. We then focus our attention on some key payoffs to investing in women in selected areas—education, employment, entrepreneurship, and political and civic engagement—highlighting just a few of the many positive examples that exist in each of these domains. We also consider the age dimension, recognizing that women face different challenges across the life cycle, and that addressing the needs of adolescent girls and the elderly (in particular widows) is critical. We close by looking ahead and identifying some of the key priorities moving forward.

Recent Trends and Patterns

Women have made unprecedented gains across a range of critical areas, including recognition of their human rights, in education, and in access to jobs and livelihoods.

At the international level we have seen some progress in recognizing women's equality and women's rights in real terms. The Convention to Eliminate All Forms of Discrimination Against Women (CEDAW), which was agreed upon in Mexico in 1975 and has been ratified by 187 countries, has been a pioneering instrument of human rights for women.[1] Progress has also been made globally in reforming legislative and constitutional frameworks to advance gender equality and women's rights—97 countries now have a nondiscrimination clause covering gender in their constitution, and 132 countries have constitutional guarantees of equality before the law (World Bank, 2012b).

In education, most countries around the world have attained gender parity in primary schooling, and women now make up more than half of the world's university students. However, there are still 35 million primary school aged girls out of school, mainly in Africa (World Bank, 2012a). Notwithstanding that overall progress on getting girls in school in Africa is evident—the average number of girls for every 100 boys in primary school in the region increased from 85 in 1999 to 91 in 2008 (World Bank, 2012a)—the region is still home to many of the countries where major gender disadvantage exists, including in Benin, Chad, Niger, and Togo.

Gender parity at secondary levels is lagging behind. Overall more boys than girls are in secondary school in most developing countries and most regions, with the exception of Central and Eastern Europe, East Asia and the Pacific, and North Africa, which have achieved gender parity at the secondary level (UNICEF, 2012). At the same time, in 45 developing countries, girls actually outnumbered boys in secondary education, including in Bangladesh, Brazil, Honduras, Lesotho, Malaysia, Mongolia, and South Africa (World Bank, 2012a).

Streaming into different educational fields remains pervasive. Females and males continue to study different disciplines—across the world, women are overrepresented in education and health, and underrepresented in engineering, manufacturing, construction, and science (see World Bank, 2012a, Table 3.1). These fields of study feed into occupational choices, which in turn can affect what women and men earn throughout their adult lives. The WDR 2012 examined 33 developing countries and found that gender differences in occupation and sector of employment accounted for between 10–50 percent of the observed gender wage gap.

With higher levels of education, a new challenge has emerged: Many girls are stalled between school and productive work. Fewer than one quarter of young women are employed in South Asia compared to 58 percent of their male peers, and only around 43 percent of young women in Latin America and the Caribbean are employed as compared to 63 percent of young men (International Labour Organisation, 2012). Indeed, the gender gap in youth labor force participation has remained largely unchanged at around 16 percent, despite progress on the education front (International Labour Organisation, 2012). This suggests that accessing education is just the first step, and that translating those gains into productive employment remains a challenge. This has serious consequences for economic development also. Recent research from the Gulf region suggests that if two million of the region's highly educated women entered paid work, the region's gross domestic product (GDP) could rise by 30 percent (or $363 billion) (Scott-Jackson, Kariem, Porteous, & Harb, 2010).

Women's labor force participation has grown markedly in the past 25 years, partially closing the gender participation gap,[2] as economic growth and expanding economic opportunities have drawn many women into the market. Today women represent 41 percent of the global labor force in the formal sector and 43 percent of the agricultural workforce (World Bank, 2012a). Yet across the world women earn less than men for similar work, and they are more likely to work in the informal economy (Fig. 1.1), in low value-added sectors, and in low-paid jobs characterized by poor working conditions (Duflo, 2011; Krogh, Hansen, Wendt, & Elkjaer, 2009). Globally, women are three times as likely as men to be hired informally and are much more likely to be unpaid workers that contribute to a family business than men (Simavi, Manual, & Blackden, 2010, p. 4).

FIGURE 1.1: EMPLOYMENT IN THE INFORMAL SECTOR AS PERCENTAGE OF TOTAL EMPLOYMENT, BY SEX

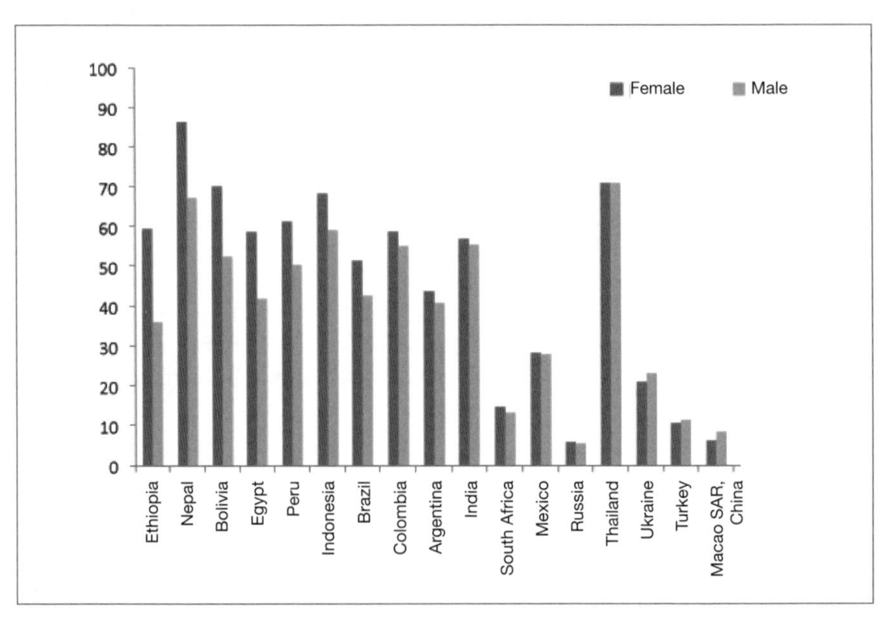

Source: World Bank (2012a, Fig. 2.6).

Women are also far more likely than men to work part-time—nearly three out of every four part-time jobs in OECD (Organisation for Economic Co-operation and Development) countries, for example, are held by women (OECD, 2008). This disparity can in part be explained by differences in the types of activities and jobs that women do, and by differences in the returns to worker and job characteristics. Women's time use and the gender division of labor within the home play into these divisions—women spend almost twice as much time on housework, almost five times as much on child care, and about half as much time on market work as men do (Berniell & Sanchez-Paramo, 2011). Flexible working arrangements, such as part-time or informal jobs, allow women to combine work with household and family obligations. Recent evidence from Spain, for example, suggests that the very high rate of part-time work by women is explained in large part by the presence of children (Peri et al., 2012).

Where women are formally employed, they tend to cluster in a small number of industrial sectors—more than one-fifth of the total female labor force is in manufacturing, and women compose more than two-thirds of the global labor force in garment production (Cuberes & Teignier-Baque, 2011). Even where women do work the same hours as men, gender pay gaps persist—notwithstanding that most countries (128 of the 141 countries included in the World Bank's *Women, Business and the Law* report) have laws requiring equal pay for equal work (World Bank, 2012b). In sub-Saharan Africa, for example, the average female-to-male weekly income gap ranges between 23 percent in Burkina Faso to 79 percent in Ghana (Kolev & Sirven, 2007).

Moving beyond education and employment, we find that progress in other areas has been slower. Progress in expanding women's agency, for example, has been limited in important respects. Agency is about the ability of individuals and groups to make effective choices—and to transform those choices into desired actions and outcomes. Women's agency influences their ability to build human capital, to take up economic opportunities, and to participate effectively in private and public life. And yet the WDR 2012 identifies this as an area where progress has been slowest.

Domestic violence, for example, remains prevalent across all regions. Violence against women both reflects and reinforces inequalities between women and men, and it damages the health, dignity, security, and autonomy of its victims. Many penal and civil law codes still fail to criminalize certain kinds of physical, sexual, or emotional violence, and even where laws are in place to protect women, social and cultural norms often prevent women from exercising those rights. As a result, domestic violence statistics around the world are horrifying[3]—at least 1 of every 10 ever-partnered women is physically or sexually assaulted by an intimate partner or someone she knows at some point in her life (World Bank, 2012a).

The share of women in political decision-making has been improving—the number of elected women heads of state and government more than doubled between 2005 and 2012, to 17 percent. But there is still a very long way to go in most countries—women currently make up just over 19 percent of parliamentarians worldwide, and in some regions their presence is even lower. In the Middle East and North Africa, for example, women are only 1 in 10 parliamentarians, and in Papua New Guinea, there is only one female parliamentarian.[4] Scandinavian countries have the highest percentage of women ministers at 48 percent, followed by the Americas at 21 percent and sub-Saharan Africa at 20 percent.[5]

In order to know whether progress is being made toward achieving gender equality, relevant indicators and monitoring are needed. This is a difficult endeavor, due in part to deficient data and the fact that some dimensions, such as agency, do not lend themselves easily to measurement. But even imperfect measures raise awareness of problems, permit monitoring of progress toward gender equity objectives, and help keep governments accountable. In this light, the Gender Inequality Index (GII), introduced in the 2010 Human Development Report, aims to capture women's disadvantage in three dimensions: empowerment, economic activity, and reproductive health (United Nations Development Programme [UNDP], 2010). The GII shows the loss in human development due to inequality between women and men in these dimensions. The results are striking.

Covering 145 countries, the 2011 estimates show that countries with lower human development tend to experience higher gender inequality, however, with tremendous variation across countries—the losses in human development due to gender inequality range from around 5 percent in Sweden to 77 percent in Yemen (Fig.1. 2).

FIGURE 1.2: GENDER INEQUALITY INDEX SCORES COMPARED TO HUMAN DEVELOPMENT INDEX SCORES

Source: UNDP 2011, Table 4.

Regionally, the largest losses due to gender equality are in sub-Saharan Africa—driven by disparities in education and from high maternal mortality and adolescent fertility rates. South Asia follows closely behind, where women lag behind men in all three dimensions, most notably in education, national parliamentary representation, and participation in the workforce. Strikingly, we also see large disparities in developed countries. The United States, for example, drops 43 places in the Human Development Index when gender inequality is taken into account, driven by large differences in men's and women's labor force participation, a relatively high adolescent fertility rate, and few women in national parliament (UNDP, 2011).

Thus while much progress has been made in advancing women's opportunities, there is some way to go. The increasingly widespread recognition of the benefits to investing in women buttresses the case for heightened policy attention by national governments and the international development community. We turn now to consider some of those payoffs.

Payoffs to Investing in Women and Girls

Productivity can be raised if women's skills and talents are used more fully. This is true for a range of economic activities, including agriculture and small business. Evidence from Ghana and Malawi, for example, suggest that if women farmers were given the same access to fertilizers and other inputs as men, maize yields would increase by almost one-sixth (World Bank, 2012a). And the UN Food and Agriculture Organization (FAO) estimates that equalizing access to productive resources between female and male farmers could increase agricultural output by as much as 2.5 to 4 percent (FAO, IFAD, & ILO, 2010). Similarly for women-owned businesses, evidence from Europe and Central Asia suggests that while enterprises owned and managed by women are smaller in terms of sales revenue than those owned or managed by men, women generate more profit per unit of sales revenue and show higher returns to scale (Sattar, 2012).

Greater control over household resources by women can enhance development prospects by changing spending patterns in ways that benefit children. Evidence from Cairo, Egypt, suggests a clear link between women receiving microcredit and an increase in the number of children in the household attending school (close to a 30 percent increase for both boys and girls; Nader, 2008). And in Ghana the share of assets and land owned by women are positively associated with higher food expenditure (Doss, 2006).

Educating Girls

Education promotes the ability of people to function and reach their potential in society. Raising education levels and literacy rates is one of the most effective investments for increasing productivity at work and home. Investments in girls' education impact their ability as women to own and operate productive businesses,[6] and differences in education (including differences in the subjects females and males study) explain a significant fraction of the variation in wages and incomes among women and men (World Bank, 2012a, Chap. 5). In their roles as mothers, women pass on educational benefits to their children—children born to educated mothers are less likely to die in infancy and are more likely to have higher birth weights and to be immunized (Strauss & Duncan, 1995; World Bank, 2012a).

Recent evidence from Sierra Leone illustrates some key ways that schooling can promote women's agency: One additional year of schooling was found to increase women's propensity to use modern contraception by almost 12 percentage points, and the propensity for being tested for HIV/AIDS by 11 percentage points. An additional year of schooling for women was also found to reduce the desired number of children by 0.34 percent, with no related change in preference found for men, and it reduced women's propensity to approve of wife beating by about 10 percentage points (Mocan & Cannonier, 2012).

Studies show that increasing returns to investment in girls' education, removing institutional constraints, or increasing household incomes can positively impact girls' enrollment. In Bangladesh, the expansion of job opportunities in the garment sector was associated with a rapid increase in girls' schooling—between 1983 and 2000, those villages within commuting distance to garment factories saw a 27 percent increase in girls' school enrolment rates (Heath & Mobarak, 2012). While in Afghanistan, communities randomly selected to receive a school saw a 50 percent overall increase in school attendance, with girls' enrollment increasing by 15 percentage points more than boys (Burde & Linden, 2010). Cash transfers conditioned on sending daughters to school can also have positive impacts on enrollment. Research from India estimated that female enrollment increased by 12 percentage points for each year of exposure to a Female Secondary School Assistance Program (Khandker, Pitt, & Fuwa, 2003), and in Cambodia a similar program resulted in a 31 percentage point increase in girls' transition from primary to lower-secondary school (Filmer & Schady, 2008).

Women's Employment

Providing income opportunities for poor women and men through wage employment or self-employment is crucial to raising incomes and overcoming poverty. Women's economic empowerment is important from both a human rights perspective, recognizing that good jobs and the freedom to work in security and dignity are basic human rights, and an economic perspective, recognizing women's economic capacities and their contribution to economic growth (Krogh et al., 2009).

Improving women's access to economic opportunities can have large impacts on productivity. Equalizing women and men farmers' access to productive resources, for example, could increase agricultural output in developing countries by 2.5 to 4 percent

(FAO, 2011). Eliminating discrimination against female managers could increase productivity per worker by 25 percent, while eliminating discrimination against women in the labor force could increase productivity by almost 40 percent (Cuberes & Teignier-Baque, 2011). Similarly, reducing barriers that prevent women from working in certain occupations or sectors could have positive effects on closing the wage and productivity gap between men and women. For example, about 15 to 20 percent of wage growth in the United States between 1960 and 2008 can be attributed to declines in labor market segregation by gender and race (Hsieh, Hurst, Jones, & Klenow, 2012). These gains can also bring wider benefits. To the extent that increased access to economic opportunities by women translates into greater control by women over household income, this will strengthen women's agency and result in additional gains for the household and, in particular, children. (For a thorough discussion of the relationship between increased control over household resources, women's agency, and the resulting benefits to households and children, see World Bank, 2011-2012a.)

Gender differences in education and work experience contribute to women's lower productivity and earnings (for further discussion, see World Bank, 2011-2012, Chap. 5). But improved educational achievements have not closed the wage gap, largely due to the significant gender differences that remain in sector and type of employment and care responsibilities. As noted above, streaming in education means that women end up in female-dominated fields characterized by lower status and lower-paying jobs (OECD, 2005). Recent research from Italy, for example, finds that the very large difference of choice of college major by females, in favor of humanities and away from math, engineering, and business, explains one-third of the gender gap in income (Peri et al., 2012).

Increasing the presence of women at the management level and on boards of directors can improve company management and corporate accountability. Female presence on the boards of Fortune 500 firms has been associated with better performance, primarily through the effect on the board's audit function. Greater presence of women on boards has also been linked to increased gender diversity in firms' senior management (World Bank, 2012a, Box 5.2).

Participation in productive work and increased incomes also have wider impacts on women's own agency and well-being—higher incomes can increase voice and bargaining power within the household and increase access to services. Greater economic opportunities can also broaden women's networks, thus expanding their sources of information and support. Women's employment can also have positive benefits for the next generation—Japanese men who are raised by working mothers are less likely to support gender division of roles, and in the United States, daughters of working mothers and wives of men whose mothers worked are significantly more likely to work (World Bank, 2012a, p. 151).

Women Entrepreneurs

Entrepreneurship is vitally important for job creation, private sector development, and wealth creation. Entrepreneurship and self-employment may also sometimes be a means of survival for those who cannot find any other means of earning an income (OECD, 2008).

Across most of the world, female-headed businesses are a minority—in East Asia and the Pacific, Europe and Central Asia, and Latin America and the Caribbean, women-owned businesses represent less than a quarter of all enterprises (20, 24, and 20 percent, respectively; Simavi et al., 2010), and the percentage is even lower in the Middle East and North Africa, Africa, and South Asia (13 percent, 10 percent, and 3 percent, respectively; Simavi et al., 2010). Women's businesses are also typically smaller and tend to be undercapitalized and have poorer access to productive inputs, including credit.

Lack of evidence on the binding constraints to the productivity and growth of women-owned businesses has limited our understanding about which interventions best address the underlying barriers to enhancing women-owned businesses. Recent work has highlighted three types of constraints. First, the external constraints: There are substantial gender-specific barriers to entrepreneurship that constrain the performance of female entrepreneurs, including difficulties in obtaining credit, in cultivating business networks, and in dealing with government and other officials. Second, gender gaps in human capital: Women choose sectors where they can utilize "female" skills because they are not as well-equipped as their male counterparts to start and grow businesses. And third, risk-aversion: Women choose sectors and businesses that require limited initial investment, where credit is supplied through informal channels (as opposed to via banks or other financial institutions), and women prefer income stability over growth (see Bardasi, Sabarwal, & Terrell, 2011). Research is underway to explore the extent to which these constraints play out in practice across different countries and regions, and to identify promising interventions.[7]

Evidence of these constraints is widespread. Fewer women have bank accounts with a formal financial institution than men do—worldwide 55 percent of men report having an account, while only 47 percent of women do. Surveys of financial literacy in OECD countries suggest that women have less understanding and confidence in making financial decisions than men—likely due to being unable to afford financial services and not being linked to mainstream business networks (OECD, 2005). And women have more difficulty accessing credit and other productive inputs than men (OECD, 2008). In Europe and Central Asia, for example, women-managed firms with more than five employees have a greater than 5 percent lower probability of securing a bank loan relative to men-managed firms, and they pay on average 0.6 percent higher interest rates for the loans they do receive (Muravyev, Talavera, & Schafer, 2009).

Removing bureaucratic and legal hurdles to investment and business activities can help enable the growth of women-run businesses. Providing joint ownership of property upon marriage, for example, increases women's ability to use land as collateral for accessing economic opportunities and credit. Progress in reforming such laws to benefit women and men equally is emerging—land certification and joint titling that has been implemented in Ethiopia since 1995, for example, has increased perceptions of tenure security among both women and men (UN-HABITAT, 2008).

Business and entrepreneurship incubators are showing some positive results. In Georgia, Mongolia, and Slovenia, business incubators have been increasing awareness around women's roles as business owners and seeking to enhance the participation of women entrepreneurs in the economy (Sattar, 2012). MKUBWA, the Tanzania Virtual Business Incubator, has empowered 500 women entrepreneurs in Dar es Salaam and Kibaha by helping them to develop entrepreneurial skills and by facilitating access to improved employment opportunities through expanded business networks and improved access to new markets.[8] Similarly, businesswomen's networks have been established in many regions to mobilize and connect women professionals and entrepreneurs, and to promote economic growth and strengthen the business environment for women's economic engagement through training, mentorship, and capacity building programs.[9]

Investing in Women's Political and Civic Engagement

There is growing recognition of the untapped capacity and talents of women as leaders and decision makers. In order for women's voices to be transformative, they need to be present where decisions are made—including in parliament, legal institutions, professional institutions, local and state governments, and informal community decision-making bodies. Women's ability to challenge the status quo also depends on their ability to speak collectively.

A 2008 survey of parliamentarians in 110 countries found that male and female legislators emphasize different priorities. In fact, more than 90 percent of all respondents agreed that women bring different views, talents, and perspectives to politics. Women tend to prioritize social issues such as child care, equal pay, parental leave, and pensions; physical concerns such as reproductive health and physical safety; and poverty reduction and service delivery (Inter-Parliamentary Union [IPU], 2008).

Notwithstanding this growing recognition, the rate of women's representation in national parliaments globally remains low. There has been a rise since 1999 from 13 to almost 20 percent, but this progress is varied across regions, and progress is not linear. In Queensland, Australia, for example, following the 2012 state elections, the proportion of women representatives sitting in parliament dropped from 37 percent of the chamber (holding 33 out of 89 seats) to a mere 20 percent (18 seats).[10]

In sub-Saharan Africa, the number of women in parliaments has risen from around 11 percent to almost 20 percent, and is much higher in some countries—women compose 56 percent of the lower house and 39 percent of the upper house in Rwanda, and 42 percent of the lower house and 32 percent of the upper house in South Africa.[11] In the Middle East and North Africa women still make up only around 1 in 10 parliamentarians, with no women in parliament in Kuwait, Qatar, and Saudi Arabia.[12] Prejudice and social norms about the role of women, along with lack of financial resources, are among major obstacles to women winning a seat in parliament (IPU, 2008).

Quotas, while controversial, can be an effective means of improving women's participation. More than half of countries worldwide have implemented some form of political quota. And in many cases they seem to have translated into higher representation of women: 17 out of the 59 countries that held elections in 2011 had legislated quotas, and women gained 27 percent of parliamentary seats in those countries, compared to 16 percent in countries without quotas (IPU, 2011).

Women's collective voices can help stimulate progress, and local women's groups appear to be increasingly effective. Protests in 2011 by activists and women's groups in Egypt, for example, with support from the Liberal Free Egyptians Party, are continuing to put sexual harassment issues into the mainstream and demanding antiharassment laws. One result of this collective action is HARASSmap, which is used to collect and locate complaints of harassment by Egyptian women and is used as evidence of the widespread nature of the problem (Hack, 2012; Power, 2012). And in the war-torn city of Mostar, Bosnia-Herzegovina, women came together across ethnic lines to build an advocacy network that uses community organizing, public outreach, and petitioning of government to bridge the city's sharp ethnic divisions and solve pressing community wide problems. These women succeeded in introducing amendments to the municipal maternity law to better protect female workers. These are courageous women who put aside harmful differences and chose the political process to build better lives for themselves and their community.[13]

The Age Dimension

Traditionally, the specific challenges facing adolescent girls as they transition into mothers, wives, and adult members of the workforce and society have been neglected. Some of the key challenges include early school dropout, early marriage, teen pregnancy, and joblessness—major events that can have repercussions for both the girls themselves and the next generation. Young girls also often face household or community perceptions that they have limited economic prospects compared to boys, which can result in reduced family incentives to keep daughters in school or to otherwise invest in their well-being.

Investing in girls is critical for development and for breaking the intergenerational cycle of poverty. The challenges adolescent girls face can result in lost opportunities for themselves and their communities. Recent cross-country analysis estimates that primary education increases girls' lifetime earnings by 5–12 percent, compared to 4–8 percent for boys (Chaaban & Cunningham, 2011). But girls also have higher rates of "inactivity" than boys across all developing countries. In some countries, including India, Nigeria, and South Africa, more than three-quarters of all girls aged 15–24 are not engaged in paid work and are not looking for work. The lifetime costs related to adolescent pregnancy can be large: Measured by a young mother's foregone income over her lifetime, these costs range from 1 percent of annual GDP in China (where the adolescent fertility rate is relatively low) to 30 percent of annual GDP in Uganda (where there are 148 births for every 1,000 girls aged 15–19; Chaaban & Cunningham, 2011).

This is an area where policy attention is now rising. In 2008, for example, the World Bank launched the Adolescent Girls Initiative, which aims to help adolescent girls and young women make a successful transition from school to work. The program is being piloted in eight countries, with the common goal of discovering what kinds of programs are most successful at helping young women succeed in the labor market. The pilots are expected to impact economic outcomes for participants and their households (such as employment, earnings, saving, and borrowing); changes in socioeconomic behaviors and outcomes (such as marriage, fertility, and time use); and empowerment and agency (such as aspirations and control over household resources) (World Bank, 2010). Similar pilot programs are underway in Tanzania and Uganda (World Bank, 2012b).

An innovative recent global initiative is the G(irls)20 Summit, which brings together one 18- to 20-year-old girl from each G20 country two weeks before the annual G20 leaders meeting. The Mexico Summit in 2012 looked at the G20 agenda through the lens of the economic empowerment of girls and women, where delegates discussed scalable solutions toward financial prosperity and the economic and political empowerment of girls and women. The summit culminated in a communiqué which emphasized that "equal access to productive resources, land and credit are all key factors in turning opportunity lost into opportunity gained as it relates to a woman's ability to be economically productive. In addition, as women represent a majority of purchasing power, it is necessary to global growth that women play a key role in decision making at every level."[14] Other global initiatives supporting girls include Girl Up[15] and Girls Learn International,[16] which complement a range of national level efforts.

At the other end of the spectrum, elderly women, and in particular widows, are another group who face specific challenges. Older women are three times as likely as older men to lose a spouse—among the elderly who do not live in an extended household, more elderly women across the world live alone, while more men live with their spouses. And upon the death of a spouse, women face significant risks of reversals in autonomy (World Bank, 2012a, Chap. 4).

Yet inheritance laws and practices are often considerably weaker for women. In 2011, 26 countries had statutory inheritance rights that differentiate between women and men (and the number would likely be much higher if we were also to include restrictions under customary laws). This includes all 14 countries from the Middle East and North Africa that are included in the *Women, Business and the Law* report, as well as seven in sub-Saharan Africa, three in South Asia, and two in East Asia and the Pacific (World Bank, 2012c). Yet even where countries reform their laws toward more equal treatment of women and men, important differences can persist. Sometimes information of the reforms is not well disseminated and/or laws may be ignored or weakly enforced, or in the case of inheritance they may be circumvented through the making of wills.

In 16 sub-Saharan African countries more than half of widows do not inherit any assets from their deceased husbands. As a result widows are less likely than male-headed households to own land—this is the case in 70 percent of the countries with data available (World Bank, 2012a, Box 4.3). In Mali, important gender differences in access and control over resources mean that women are highly dependent on men—first fathers, then husbands, and if widowed, adult sons. This makes Malian women particularly vulnerable in the case of loss of a husband. Research suggests that households headed by widows have significantly lower living standards than all other male- or female-headed households; that even upon remarriage, widows have lower welfare relative to other women; and that these detrimental effects are passed on to children (Van de Walle, 2011).

Globally, inheritance reforms in favor of daughters have been more advanced than reforms to strengthen the rights of widows. This is partly linked to the underlying presumption that male relatives are obliged to take care of dependent female relatives, although in reality this is often not the case. Widow pensions have been introduced in a number of countries, such as India, where targeted unconditional cash transfers in a number of states reach around 3 million widows, and are showing increasingly positive results (Dutta, Howes, & Murgani, 2010).

Yet it is also true that in some cases widowhood can actually open up freedoms and opportunities. This is particularly the case where marriage is associated with social, economic, and physical restrictions. In Afghanistan, for example, widows ranked high on the scale of power and rights in the WDR 2012 qualitative study, because they took over decision-making power within the household and were able to have independent economic activities, and in the Republic of Yemen widows had greater freedom of mobility in order to work to provide for their families (World Bank, 2012a, Box 4.3).

Looking Ahead

It is clear that there has been much progress in expanding women's endowments, opportunities, and agency. Investing in women has clear benefits for women and their families, as well as for broader economic and social development.

But there is still a long way to go. There are missing gender dimensions of poverty that are not well captured by existing quantitative research—including time use and agency. The dearth of gender disaggregated data in many areas is also a limiting factor to effective and impactful investments in women.

In 2012, gender equality and investing in women is firmly on the agenda of the international development community—including as one of the World Bank's priority areas. The key priorities now include building a strong knowledge base and filling gaps in data and evidence to inform the way forward.

NOTES

[1] http://treaties.un.org/Pages/ViewDetails.aspx?src=TREATY&mtdsg_no=IV-8&chapter=4&lang=en

[2] Between 1980 and 2009, the global rate of female labor force participation rose from 50.2 percent to 51.8 percent, while the male rate fell from 82 percent to 77.7 percent—consequently the gender participation gap declined from 32 percentage points in 1980 to 26 percentage points in 2009 (World Bank, 2011–2012, Box 5.1).

[3] The dearth of reliable data on domestic violence in most countries, due in part to limited reporting of incidents by victims, impedes the policy and advocacy work necessary to address this issue.

[4] Inter-Parliamentary Union: http://ipu.org

[5] Regional groupings are based on IPU PARLINE Geographical Groupings (IPU, 2012,Women in Politics 2012: http://www.ipu.org/pdf/publications/wmnmap12_en.pdf

[6] Results from Sub-Saharan Africa imply that improving women's education—including business skills—could help raise the relative productivity of women entrepreneurs (Aterido & Hallward-Driemeier, 2009).

[7] The World Bank is using funds provided by USAID to provide technical assistance and financial incentives to World Bank project teams to incorporate pilot interventions to enhance women's leadership in ongoing projects that are relevant to the WLSME program

[8] http://siteresources.worldbank.org/INTGENDER/Resources/RBI_briefs.pdf

[9] For example, see Vital Voices Global Partnership: http://www.vitalvoices.org/what-we-do/regions/latin-america-and-caribbean/lac-businesswomens-network

[10] http://girlsgerms.com.au/2012/03/29/gender-divide-in-qld-politics-just-got-deeper/

[11] IPU. Accessed on June 5, 2012: http://ipu.org/wmn-e/classif.htm#1

[12] IPU. Accessed on May 31, 2012: http://ipu.org

[13] The National Democratic Institute: Bosnian women healing wounded city. http://www.ndi.org/node/14125

[14] http://www.girls20summit.com/wp-content/uploads/2012-MEXICO-COMMUNIQUE_FINAL.pdf

[15] http://www.girlup.org/

[16] http://girlslearn.net/

REFERENCES

Aterido, R., & Hallward-Driemeier, M. (2009). Whose business is it anyway? Washington, DC: World Bank.

Bardasi, E., Sabarwal, S., & Terrell, K. (2011). How do female entrepreneurs perform? Evidence from three developing regions. *Small Business Economics*, 37(4), 417–441. Retrieved from http://link.springer.com/article/10.1007%2Fs11187-011-9374-z?LI=true#page-1

Berniell, M. I., & Sanchez-Paramo, C. (2011). *Overview of time use data for the analysis of gender differences in time use patterns* (Background Paper for WDR 2012).

Burde, D., & Linden, L. L. (2010). *The effect of village-based schools: Evidence from a RCT in Afghanistan* (NYU Steinhardt Working Paper). Retrieved from http://economics.stanford.edu/files/Linden3_30.pdf

Chaaban, J., & Cunningham, W. (2011). *Measuring the economic gain of investing in girls: The girl effect dividend* (Policy Research Working Paper 5753). Washington DC: World Bank.

Cuberes, D., & Teignier-Baque, M. (2011). *Gender inequality and economic growth* (Background Paper for the WDR 2012).

Doss, C. (2006). The effect of intrahousehold property ownership on spending patterns in Ghana. *Journal of Africa Economies, 15*(1), 1–25.

Duflo, E. (2011). *Women's empowerment and economic development* (NBER Working Paper Series 17702). Cambridge, MA: MIT. Retrieved from http://economics.mit.edu/files/7417

Dutta, P., Howes, S., & Murgani, R. (2010). *Small but effective: India's targeted unconditional cash transfers* (ASARC Working Paper 2010/18). Retrieved from http://www.crawford.anu.edu.au/acde/asarc/pdf/papers/2010/WP2010_18.pdf

Food and Agriculture Organization, International Fund for Agricultural Development, & International Labour Office. (2010). "Gender Dimensions of Agricultural and Rural Employment: Differentiatied Pathways out of Poverty Status, Trends and Gaps." FAO, IFAD and ILO: Rome, Italy.

Filmer, D., & Schady, N. (2008). *Getting girls into school: Evidence from a scholarship program in Cambodia* (Policy Research Working Paper 3910). Washington, DC: World Bank. Retrieved from http://siteresources.worldbank.org/INTPUBSERV/Resources/477250-1186007634742/Filmer&SchadyGettingGirlsSchool.pdf

Food and Agriculture Organization (FAO). (2011). *The state of food and agriculture 2010–2011. Women in agriculture: Closing the gender gap for development.* Rome, Italy: Food and Agriculture Organization.

Hack, A. (2012, February 1). On the revolution's anniversary, men stand up for women's rights in Egypt. *Today's Zaman.* Retrieved from http://www.todayszaman.com/newsDetail_getNewsById.action?newsId=270235

Heath, R., & Mobarak, A. M. (2012). *Does demand or supply constrain investments in education? Evidence from garment sector jobs in Bangladesh* (Working Paper). Retrieved from http://faculty.som.yale.edu/mushfiqmobarak/garments.pdf

Hsieh, C-T., Hurst, E., Jones, C., & Klenow, P. J. (2012). *The allocation of talent and U.S. economic growth* (Working Paper). Retrieved from http://klenow.com/HHJK.pdf

International Labour Organisation. (2012). *Global employment trends for youth 2012*. Retrieved from http://www.ilo.org/global/research/global-reports/global-employment-trends/youth/2012/WCMS_180976/lang—en/index.htm

Inter-Parliamentary Union (IPU). (2008). *Equality in politics: A survey of men and women in parliaments*. Geneva, Switzerland: IPU. Retrieved from http://www.ipu.org/pdf/publications/equality08-e.pdf

Inter-Parliamentary Union (IPU). (2011). *Women in parliament 2011: The year in perspective*. Retrieved from http://www.ipu.org/pdf/publications/wmnpersp11-e.pdf

Khandker, S., Pitt, M., & Fuwa, N. (2003). *Subsidy to promote girls' secondary education: The female stipend program in Bangladesh* (MPRA Paper No. 23688). Retrieved from http://mpra.ub.uni-muenchen.de/23688/1/MPRA_paper_23688.pdf

Kolev, A., & Sirven, N. (2007). *Gender disparities in Africa's labor markets: A cross-country comparison using standardized survey data.* (Study prepared as part of a joint research project by the French Development Agency, Paris, and the World Bank, Washington, DC). In J. S. Arbache, A. Kolev, & E. Filipiak (Eds.), *Gender disparities in Africa's labor market* (pp. 23–54). Washington, DC: World Bank. Retrieved from http://africaknowledgelab.worldbank.org/akl/sites/africaknowledgelab.worldbank.org/files/GDALM_Full_Report.pdf

Krogh, E., Hansen, T. N., Wendt, S., & Elkjaer, M. (2009). Promoting employment for women as a strategy for poverty reduction. In OECD (Ed.), *Promoting pro-poor growth: Employment*. Paris, France: OECD.

Mocan, N. H., & Cannonier, C. (2012). *Empowering women through education: Evidence from Sierra Leone* (NBER Working Paper Series 18016). Retrieved from http://www.nber.org/papers/w18016

Muravyev, A., Talavera, O., & Schafer, D. (2009). Entrepreneurs' gender and financial constraints: Evidence from international data. *Journal of Comparative Economics 37*(2), 270–286.

Nader, Y. (2008). Microcredit and the socio-economic wellbeing of women and their families in Cairo. *Journal of Socio-Economics 37*, 644–656.

OECD (2005). *Improving financial literacy*. Paris, France: OECD.

OECD (2008). *Gender and Sustainable Development: Maximizing the economic, social and environmental role of women*. Retrieved from http://www.oecd.org/dataoecd/58/1/40881538.pdf

Peri, G., Anelli, M., de la Rica, S., de San Roman, A., Flabbi, L., & Tajeda, M. (2012). The wage gap in the transition from school to work. *Adapt Bulletin, 22*. Retrieved from http://www.frdb.org/upload/file/Report1_May_25_2012.pdf

Power, C. (2012, June 4). The price of sexism. *Time Magazine*. Retrieved from http://www.time.com/time/magazine/article/0,9171,2115647,00.html

Sattar, S. (2012). *Opportunities for men and women: Emerging Europe and Central Asia*. Washington DC: World Bank. Retrieved from http://siteresources.worldbank.org/ECAEXT/Resources/258598-1322580725430/WB_gender_report_EXE_SUM_11_21_11.pdf

Scott-Jackson, W., Kariem, B., Porteous, A., & Harb, A. (2010). *Maximizing women's participation in the GCC workforce*. Oxford Strategic Consulting, Gulf. Retrieved from http://www.academia.edu/554086/Maximising_Womens_participation_in_the_GCC_workforce

Sen, A. (1989). Development as capability expansion. *Journal of Development Planning, 17*, 41–58.

Simavi, S., Manual, C., & Blackden, M. (2010). *Gender dimensions of investment climate reform: A guide for policy makers and practitioners*. Washington, DC: World Bank.

Strauss, J., & Duncan, T. (1995). Human resources: Empirical modeling of household and family decisions. In J. Behrman & T. N. Srinivasan (Eds.), *Handbook of Development Economics, Vol. 3*. Retrieved from http://EconPapers.repec.org/RePEc:eee:devhes:3

UNDP. (2010). *Human development report: The real wealth of nations*. New York, NY: United Nations Development Program.

UNDP. (2011). *Human development report: Sustainability and equity, a better future for all.* New York, NY: United Nations Development Program.

UN-HABITAT. (2008). *Land registration in Ethiopia: Early impacts on women.* Nairobi, Kenya: United Nations-HABITAT.

UNICEF. (2012, April 2012). *Progress for children: A report card on adolescents.* Number 10. http://www.unicef.org/publications/files/Progress_for_Children_-_No._10_EN_04232012.pdf

United Nations. (2005). *Progress towards the Millennium Development Goals, 1990–2005. Secretary General's Millennium Development Goals Report, June 13, 2005.*

Van de Walle, D. (2011). *Welfare effects of widowhood in a poor country.* Washington, DC: World Bank.

World Bank. (2012a). *World development report 2012: Gender equality and development.* Washington, DC: World Bank.

World Bank. (2012b). *Women, business and the law.* Washington, DC. World Bank.

Chapter Two

WOMEN AS SOCIAL ENTREPRENEURS: A CASE STUDY

NÜKET KARDAM, MONTEREY INSTITUTE OF INTERNATIONAL STUDIES

FREDRIC KROPP, MONTEREY INSTITUTE OF INTERNATIONAL STUDIES

Introduction

The rise of women's global networks and activities around the world has been widely studied since the mid-1970s. Women's leadership is pivotal in spearheading social change at local, national, and global levels. Such leadership is generally exercised through civil society and nongovernmental organizations, with the assistance and partnership of many donors (Kardam, 2004). There is also evidence that the pressure of individual activists, women's groups, and women-led organizations put pressure on their own governments from the bottom up, as well through global organizing efforts under UN auspices (Alvarez, 2000; Kardam, 2004). These women leaders are change agents who contribute strongly to shaping global women's human rights and gender equality norms, along with promoting legal reforms and their implementation on gender equality at national and local levels. In all of these activities, the mission has been to empower women and to promote greater justice for women.

Two different and complementary approaches have served this broad mission: policy advocacy and entrepreneurship. Advocacy requires specific skills and strategies, compiling "expert" information to support one's political claims or desired policy changes. It involves knowing how to argue a case, possessing political know-how, lobbying, and forming alliances and partnerships. Effective leaders are characterized as entrepreneurs or brokers who use skill, ingenuity, and creativity, rather than power to present issues and create new institutional options (Young, 1991). The word *entrepreneur* has more recently been applied not just to "social activists" who act as policy entrepreneurs, but also to those people who focus on achieving social missions through entrepreneurial approaches.

Although businesses and nonprofit organizations have performed socially oriented activities for many years, social entrepreneurship is a relatively new field. Early definitions refer to social entrepreneurs as change agents (Dees, 2001; Seelos & Mair, 2005) who try to solve social problems through pattern-breaking change (Light, 2008). Dees (2001) elaborated on the concept of social entrepreneurs as change agents since they identify opportunities and create mission-based vehicles to create and sustain social value. Building on these concepts, Zahra, Gedajlovic, Neubaum, & Shulman (2009) identified that social entrepreneurship "encompasses the activities and processes undertaken to discover, define, and exploit opportunities in order to enhance social wealth by creating new ventures or managing existing organizations in an innovative manner" (p. 519).

This chapter focuses on a small set of women social entrepreneurs in order to investigate their motivations, explanations for their success, and characteristics that may be based on their gender. The aim of this chapter is to contribute to the discussion of the potential and real contributions of women social entrepreneurs to social change. In a report on social entrepreneurship in 2009, the Global Entrepreneurship Monitor (GEM) project interviewed 150,000 adults in 49 countries and found that an average of 2.8 percent of the world's working population was involved in socially oriented activities (Terjesen, Lepoutre, Justo, & Bosma, 2011). The report showed a wide range of variation by country, ranging from a low of 0.02 percent in Malaysia to a high of 7.6 percent in Argentina. In general, the Middle East and North Africa are far below the global average. Though men are more likely to start ventures than women, the gap is much lower in social entrepreneurship than in commercial entrepreneurship; in fact, in some countries like Malaysia, Russia, Argentina, and Israel, more women start social ventures than men (Terjesen et al., 2011). The increasing role of women in social entrepreneurship activities presents some interesting questions. Are women different from men in terms of their approach to social change and in their practice of social entrepreneurship? Are there some specific motivational factors and explanations for success that are gender specific? How do women acting as social entrepreneurs contribute to overall social change?

We examine some of the key definitional issues of social entrepreneurship and the different categories of social entrepreneurship, and then explore some case studies of women social entrepreneurs. We draw preliminary conclusions from the factors that motivate women social entrepreneurs, as well as some challenges they face. The chapter ends with a discussion of the lessons learned and the potential and real contributions of women social entrepreneurs to overall social change.

What Is Social Entrepreneurship?

The field of social entrepreneurship has gained wider recognition over the past 10 years for several reasons. First, the growth in social entrepreneurship matches the rapid growth of entrepreneurship itself. Examining 54 economies around the world in 2011, GEM estimated that 388 million entrepreneurs were either starting or running new businesses (Kelley, Singer, & Herrington, 2012). More jobs are created through entrepreneurial activity than all other approaches combined. In the United States, for example, nearly six million people start a business each year (Kropp, Lindsay, & Hancock, 2011).

Women are increasingly becoming entrepreneurs as a part of this trend. In a different GEM study that examined 59 economies representing 52 percent of the world's population and 84 percent of the world's gross domestic product (GDP), GEM estimated that 104 million women were actively starting ventures and an additional 83 million had launched ventures at least three-and-a-half years before (Kelley, Brush, Greene, & Litovsky, 2011). The participation rate of women as entrepreneurs varies according to country, from a low of 1.5 percent of women in the working age population to a high of 45.4 percent; the proportion of entrepreneurs who are women range from 16 percent in Korea to 55 percent in Ghana (Kelley et al., 2011). In fact, women are considered the drivers of growth in Africa through cross-border trade throughout sub-Saharan Africa: selling used clothes and tin kitchenware, as hair stylists and owners of fashion salons, and running small food stores. According to the World Bank, the rate of female entrepreneurship is higher in Africa than anywhere else in the world (Kron, 2012).

Another reason for the rapid growth in social entrepreneurship is the changing role of government in many countries. Both as a function of ideology and of resource scarcity, many governments around the world decreased social welfare spending, which means that social needs will go unmet unless filled by others (Roper & Cheney, 2005). Changing norms resulted in a shift from the public sector to the private sector and the third sector in filling these unmet needs (Haugh, 2005). The *third sector* includes social entrepreneurs, philanthropic and voluntary organizations, churches, nonprofits, and community organizations (Shaw & Carter, 2007). Social entrepreneurs are particularly important as they find solutions for social problems using market-based approaches (Zahra et al., 2009).

Often many people think of *regular* or *commercial* entrepreneurship as starting a business. However, it is much more than that. Entrepreneurship is a process and describes a way that individuals and firms behave. Entrepreneurship can take place in new or existing businesses, ranging from small-scale start-ups to well-established, large multinational corporations. On the individual level, traits often associated with entrepreneurs include a proactive personality; a need for achievement, passion, perseverance, hard work, and autonomy; and a belief in one's own ability (Rauch & Frese, 2007). On the firm or organizational level, an entrepreneurial orientation refers to the processes, practices, and decision-making activities associated with entrepreneurship and is conceptualized as containing five components: proactiveness, innovativeness, a willingness to take risks, autonomy, and competitive aggressiveness (Lumpkin & Dess, 1996).

Many of the traits attributed to commercial entrepreneurship also apply to social entrepreneurship. Though most people agree that the key component of social entrepreneurship is the focus on the social mission, there is a lack of consensus on the definition of social entrepreneurship. As is often the case with a new field or discipline, social entrepreneurship is going through a sorting-out process and is struggling with defining itself. Definitions range from the overly embracing—in which everything is social entrepreneurship—to overly restrictive definitions that eliminate many aspects of social entrepreneurship.

A major quality that distinguishes social entrepreneurs is the focus on social mission. Zahra et al. (2009), building on the work of Hayak (1945), Kirzner (1973), and Schumpeter (1932,1945), developed a typology of three categories of social entrepreneurs: social *bricoleurs*, social constructionists, and social engineers. The French anthropologist Claude Levi-Strauss introduced the term *bricolage* to bridge the gap between the mythical and scientific worlds, and he described it as "making do with what is at hand" (Levi-Strauss, 1967, p. 17; Di Domenico, Haugh, & Tracey, 2010). There is no direct translation for the French word *bricolage*. However, if you were to search on the word *bricoleur* in an e-dictionary, one of the terms that often comes up is "handyman" or "handywoman" (*Reverso*, n.d.). In many ways social bricoleurs act as handymen. Typically, they identify and act upon locally-discovered opportunities to address or solve small-scale local problems.

Social constructionists tend to work on larger-scale problems and try to work though the existing social structures, instigating reform as appropriate. Social engineers are more the revolutionaries who find it difficult to work within the system and need to radically change the existing structures. In some ways social constructionists can be seen as *evolutionaries* and social engineers as *revolutionaries* who engage in creative destruction. Zahra et al. (2009) cited Jacqueline Novogratz, founder of the Acumen Fund, as an exemplar of a social constructionist.

Novogratz founded the Acumen Fund in 2001, a nonprofit venture fund that uses entrepreneurial approaches to solve the problems of global poverty. The fund provides support in the form of loans and equity investments, as well as management assistance and connection to broader social networks of entrepreneurs who are focused on delivering critical affordable goods and services such as water, healthcare, and housing. Acumen targets its philanthropic "investments" to entrepreneurs and organizations that are "focused on offering critical services—water, health, housing, and energy—at affordable prices to people earning less than four dollars a day" (Acumen Fund, n.d.). Acumen's "few big bets" receive support in the form of loans and equity investments, supplemented by management assistance and connection to broader resource networks.

Mohammad Yunis is an exemplar of another kind of social entrepreneur, a social engineer, according to Zahra et al. (2009). Yunis won the Nobel Prize for starting the Grameen Bank, a microfinance organization and a community development bank, providing loans to the poor, with a particular emphasis on women. It became so successful that it has spread within Bangladesh, where it was founded, and then to many countries around the world. Both social constructionists and engineers try to implement large-scale transformational benefits for a significant segment of society or to society at large.

As the vast majority of social entrepreneurs are bricoleurs and their impact is local (Yitshaki & Kropp, 2011), we first focus on social bricoleurs who typically work with disadvantaged groups that have limited capacity to help themselves. In addition to the sheer number of social bricoleurs, the act of bricolage is well aligned with the type of grassroots, often women-led, social entrepreneurship that has a dynamic impact on improving the lives of both women and men around the world. Even though their activities may be local, collectively, social bricoleurs have the potential to change the way we think and behave about their chosen areas, whether it is education, human rights, healthcare, poverty alleviation, environmental mitigation the arts, or any other sector in which they engage.

As indicated earlier, accomplishing the social mission is a prime focus of social entrepreneurs. Profit in and of itself is not bad, as it provides the means for a social entrepreneur to better fill her or his mission and allows for sustainability of the social enterprise. It allows the social entrepreneur to help people who could otherwise not help themselves because of a lack of financial, social, political, or other resources. Social entrepreneurs are not after short-term profits, but long-term social benefits. Consistent with the mission-based approach, Martin and Osberg (2007, p. 35) outlined three key components to social entrepreneurship:

1 Identifying a stable but inherently unjust equilibrium that causes the marginalization, or suffering of a segment of humanity that lacks the financial means or political clout to achieve any transformative benefit on its own

2 Identifying an opportunity in this unjust equilibrium, developing a social value proposition, and bringing to bear inspiration, creativity, direct action, courage, and fortitude, thereby challenging the stable state's hegemony

3 Forging a new, stable equilibrium that releases trapped potential or alleviates the suffering of the targeted group and, through imitation and the creation of a stable ecosystem, ensuring a better future for the targeted group and even society at large.

The elements of the Martin and Osberg definition are consistent with the concept of social bricolage. In colloquial terms, social bricoleurs identify a problem, try to figure out a way to fix it, and take action.

What Motivates Social Entrepreneurs?

There are many ways of looking at motivation. One is to divide it into drive theories and incentive theories. Drive theories suggest that there is an internal stimulus that motivates people, whereas incentive theory implies that individuals seek an end point (Carsud & Brannback, 2011). Drive theory is compatible with the concept of intrinsic rewards, in which an individual is motivated by internal rewards. Incentive theory is more compatible with extrinsic or external rewards.

Earlier research for starting a business tended to be economically driven (e.g., Schumpeter, 1934). Research on the internal motivations of commercial entrepreneurs identifies several factors including the need for achievement, risk taking, tolerance for ambiguity, self-efficacy, locus of control, goal setting, independence, drive, and egoistic passion (Shane, Locke, & Collins, 2003). Kropp, Lindsay, and Shoham (2006) identified other personal goals, such as the desire to be innovative or independent, and other lifestyle reasons.

The *Global Entrepreneurship Monitor: 2011 Global Report* (Kelley et al., 2012) identified three categories of economic activity: factor-driven economies where economic development is driven by basic requirements, efficiency-driven economies where governments tend to focus on proper functioning of the market, and innovation-driven economies where economic growth and job creation occur through technical innovation. Women in factor-driven economies are more likely to perceive opportunities, have the confidence to pursue them, and become entrepreneurs than women in more advanced categories of economic development (Kelley et al., 2011).

Although there are many similarities, there are significant differences between commercial and social entrepreneurship. Although commercial entrepreneurs can have socially oriented missions, the social mission is typically secondary. For social entrepreneurs, the social mission is primary (Carsud & Brannback, 2011), and social entrepreneurs try to maximize social rather than financial returns (Sullivan Mort, Weerawardena, & Carnegie, 2003). Social entrepreneurs are motivated to change attitudes and behaviors (London and Morfopoulos, 2010). Social ventures often have a spiritual or virtuous dimension (Sullivan Mort et al., 2003). Though there are significant differences among countries, in general, there are higher proportions of female social entrepreneurs than female commercial entrepreneurs. Also, there are generally more female social entrepreneurs than male, especially in Africa, and in only one country, Ghana, were there more female commercial entrepreneurs than male. In the United States, the number of male and female social entrepreneurs is approximately equal (Terjesen et al., 2011).

There is a great richness to what motivates social bricoleurs, and their motivations are quite different. In the next section, we examine a group of women social bricoleurs, followed by a section on some women social entrepreneurs who may be called social constructionists and social engineers, that is, those who try to implement large-scale transformational benefits for a significant segment of society or to society at large.

Women as Social Bricoleurs

As indicated earlier, social bricoleurs typically work with disadvantaged groups who have limited capacity to help themselves. Even though their activities may be local, collectively, social bricoleurs have the potential to change the way we think and act. What differentiates social bricoleurs from other social service providers is that they find unique ways to identify local opportunities, find resources, and deliver services to the disadvantaged. Social bricoleurs, according to Zahra et al. (2009) are especially clever in assembling and deploying resources in pursuit of their chosen causes.

Cecilia De Mello e Souza (2008) studied female grassroots leaders in Rio de Janeiro (who fit the general definition of social bricoleurs here) and identified how women may differ from their male counterparts. Her research drew on a successful network of 134 community-based organizations in Rio de Janeiro, called the Network of Healthy Communities (NHC). Given that 68 percent of the leaders of the NHC were women, De Mello e Souza examined gender-specific ways in which grassroots leaders achieve recognition for their work and their different leadership styles.

De Mello e Souza concluded that "women leaders readily fill the gap in their communities left by the absence of the state, effectively work across development sectors, and at individual, community and international levels" (De Mello e Souza, 2008, p. 482). In our view, the grassroots leaders De Mello e Souza studied are comparable to social bricoleurs because they were engaged in improving life in the favelas by (a) acting as social workers in crises; (b) improving living conditions through multiple activities that included job training, homework assistance to children, giving advice on HIV prevention, running sports and cultural activities for youth, and establishing daycare and computer centers; and (c) partnerships, participation in forums, representing their communities in City Councils and other organizations, working with local businesses, and bargaining with politicians.

Even though De Mello e Souza's research was based on a particular locale and network of organizations, the conclusions she drew on the gender-specific motivations of grassroots leaders are very relevant in understanding the motivations of women social entrepreneurs in general. Below are some of her conclusions on how women may differ from their male counterparts:

1 Many women leaders focus on children and youth as a way of extending their concerns for their own children to others.

2 They are moved by the problems of their communities and disturbed by extreme poverty and injustice.

3 They point to the absence of government initiatives and the need for basic services.

4 Women leaders are personally motivated by opportunities to move beyond community borders.

5 Women are completely devoted to activism; they typically do not limit the scope or terms of their work, and they try to attend to all demands and opportunities.

6 Women are not afraid to reveal need: "I am bold, I don't know, but I will try because I want to learn. It is no shame not to know. I am not obliged to know everything" (De Mello e Souza, 2008, p. 489).

7 Women are eager to reach people, are uninhibited in trying new strategies, and forge informal networks.

8 Women undertake various different projects and initiatives at the same time, which means they can benefit from potential synergies with the others.

9 Women are less threatened by the possibility of failure and more willing to experiment.

Female social bricoleurs identify a social need, see it as an opportunity for change, bring to bear their expertise, marshal the necessary resources, and deliver new services for the disadvantaged. What differentiates them as women may be that most of them focus on families, women, youth, and children. Also, pull factors such as events related to family, how they were brought up, ideological orientations of their families, and life-changing events are often more important motivators than push factors. Women social bricoleurs also share the common characteristic of being strong communicators and networkers. They are willing to experiment, forge new networks and new partnerships, and try new strategies, while male leaders often tend to rely more on traditional strategies and formal political channels. Women may, however, tend toward trying too many strategies at one time, over-networking, or becoming involved in multiple projects and initiatives at the same time, while men typically focus on one enterprise at a time. Women also often rely on whatever resources are readily harnessed, which may make it difficult in the long run to sustain operations and expand.

Social Constructionists

Social bricoleurs deal with local small-scale problems; social constructionists aim to develop more formal and systemic solutions that could be transferred to different social contexts. Social constructionists build, launch, and operate ventures that tackle social needs that are inadequately addressed by existing institutions, businesses, NGOs, and government agencies. They find unique ways to generate social wealth by creating and reconfiguring the processes to deliver goods and services (Zahra et al., 2009). Both social constructionists and social engineers try to implement large-scale transformational benefits for a significant segment of society or to society at large.

Female social constructionists tend to build bridges to connect technology, business acumen, local needs, as well as among networks that may otherwise not be accessible to each other.

Michaela Walsh helped to found Women's World Banking (WWB) in 1970, an organization that helps to support and organize women-led banks and financial institutions, offering direct services to some of the poorest women in the world. WWB reaches poor women who otherwise would not have access to loans and puts women in decision-making positions. It has affiliates in countries across Asia, Africa, the Middle East, and North America, and it has provided financial services of about $18.5 billion in direct credit to more than 18 million women.

Katherine Lucy adopted an unlikely business model to Uganda. Using the model of cosmetics company Avon (women are extended a loan by providing them with inventory), Lucy established Solar Sister to distribute solar energy in Uganda, Sudan, and Rwanda (Chhabra, 2011). Lucy spent 20 years as an investment banker, but eventually grew restless at home and started looking for ways to get back to work. She was focused on the energy sector and settled on the idea of providing solar-powered energy to Uganda. That is when the idea of Solar Sister came about. The organization works to provide women with planning and materials to sell solar-powered lanterns to replace the kerosene lamps. Originally, solar panels were being used, but women were not comfortable with that technology. Lucy decided to close that gender gap by developing the idea of solar lamps—very intuitive to use, affordable, and not as "techie" as solar panels. The solar lanterns are cheaper and easier to use, and they empower the women by promoting their entrepreneurship. In fact, Lucy found out that women make the best sales force in rural Africa because they are the ones who deal with friends and neighbors, thus creating the most effective distribution channel to rural and hard-to-reach customers (Chhabra).

Vera Cordeiro, a physician in Rio de Janeiro, is the founder of *Renascer* (Rebirth: Association for Children's Health), the flagship in a network of organizations that extends care to poor children after they are discharged from public hospitals. Cordeiro was moved by the extreme poverty and injustice in the favelas, comparing the wealth of her family with the poverty of children she saw as a doctor. As a child, she was also acutely aware of the differences between her family and their neighbors. Cordeiro identified the absence of government services and the need for basic services in this area. She founded *Renascer* in 1991, and by 2007 she had extended her work to 16 public hospitals in Rio de Janeiro, Sao Paolo, and Recife, bringing direct benefits to more than 20,000 children. Cordeiro was undeterred in the face of rejection and criticism. When she presented a proposal and was told "this is government's work," she spent the next six months persuading staff in the pediatric unit to help her. "She brought together 50 colleagues in the playground of her apartment building, announced her plan, and raffled off a set of sheets that her mother had embroidered. The $100 they raised was used to cover the incorporation fees of Renascer" (Bornstein, 2007, p. 133).

Jerro Billimoria, another social constructionist, set up a hotline called Childline to assist children in distress in India. Millions of children in India live on the streets and work as underage laborers. Billimoria imagined emergency calls ringing into a hotline reporting cases such as injuries, abuse, abandonment, assault, and AIDS. She succeeded in partnering with the police departments in Bombay, creating a hotline that is now institutionalized in 42 cities across India. A new national child protection system is being created. Billimoria was motivated by the poverty and injustice and her family experience. She grew up in a prominent Bombay family in which the dominant profession was accounting. She was influenced by her father: "My father was a very kind man. He felt very strongly that you should focus on giving of yourself. And I found out after his death, despite his being so unwell—he had a heart and lung condition—that he had helped many people living on the street anonymously. We had queues of people who came to pay their respects" (Bornstein, 2007, p. 77). Billimoria continuously experimented, networked, and didn't take no for an answer. She had a mission, to create a national child protection system. Asked about the most important challenge she faced, she replied, "If I have to summarize it in one line, it would be learning to let go. Everything will not be exactly the way you want it. You have to let people take charge. Anyway, I don't take ownership for Childline. It happens because it has to happen. Not because of me" (Bornstein, p. 91).

It seems that women entrepreneurs like Walsh and Novogratz, with a business background and based in Western countries, may have a greater tendency to run their organizations as a business with a clearer separation of public and private roles, while Cardeiro in Brazil and Billimoria in India have a style that combines public and private roles, social activism and multitasking, to the point that they are very much consumed by their mission and separating themselves from the social mission may be a problem.

So then what are some of the common factors that have led to women's success as social constructionists? They, like men, are motivated by market failures and are alert to opportunities to fill the gaps to underserved clients. They seek to contribute to the reforms and innovations of the broader social system and address an ongoing social need in an effort to institutionalize social change. However, female social entrepreneurs share some common characteristics. Typically, female social entrepreneurs are focused on family-, women-, and youth-related issues. They are also mostly motivated by pull factors, including their family experiences and the injustices they have witnessed. At the same time, there are social constructionists such as Michaela Walsh and Katherine Lucy, who successfully worked in the business world and want to apply what they have learned to help alleviate social problems. They can be well-educated and/or privileged and can bring together knowledge, skills, and resources from different locations to solve a specific problems. They are able to draw people to them, inspire them with their vision, and convince them of the importance of the mission, putting themselves and their egos in the background.

Social Engineers

Social engineers go one step beyond social constructionists by introducing revolutionary change. They do not feel that they can accomplish the social change they want to bring about within the existing system. They destroy in order to rebuild, and by their very existence constitute a threat to the power holders, and therefore may be seen as illegitimate. It is possible to think of social constructionists and engineers as people who formulate a vision to change existing power relations in the long term—a vision that captures others' imagination. They are motivated to reform existing institutions and create new, sustainable ones. For example, Dame Anita Roddick founded The Body Shop, a cosmetics company producing and retailing beauty products that shaped ethical consumerism. The company was one of the first to prohibit the use of ingredients tested on animals and one of the first to promote fair trade with developing countries.

Florence Nightingale is a historical example of a social engineer. She is famous for laying the foundations of professional nursing with the establishment of her nursing school at St. Thomas' Hospital in London. Her social reforms include improving healthcare for all sections of British society, improving healthcare and advocating for better hunger relief in India, helping to abolish laws regulating prostitution, and expanding the acceptable forms of female labor participation.

Victoria Hale and Carmel Jud are two current examples of social engineers. Hale is the founder of One World Health, the first nonprofit pharmaceutical company in the United States. Her passion is the development of important new medicines for humanity with the specific goal to reduce health inequities. Under her leadership, One World Health developed a new cure for visceral leishmaniasis, also known as black fever or dumdum fever, which is the second most prevalent parasitic killer in the world. One World Health also launched a novel approach to treat dehydrating diarrhea, and it developed technology to reduce the cost of malaria drugs by more than 10-fold (http://www.medicines360.org/about-us/leadership/bios/victoria-hale-phd-ceo-founder). Carmel Jud, of Rising International (see http://www.rising international.org), promotes ownership of craft-based businesses by women in impoverished areas of developed nations, as well as in developing nations, with a focus on women in high-risk environments such as those in refugee camps, those living with HIV/AIDS, homeless women, displaced immigrants, former slaves, or those in war-torn regions of the world. The crafts are imported into other countries, where they are sold at house parties. The unique twist is that the sales representatives are also at-risk women who are trained to be successful in sales. Although it is in its early stages, Rising International has helped women in 45 countries.

Conclusions

Although there are many common characteristics shared by both female and male social entrepreneurs, such as a focus on social mission, ability to identify an opportunity, and resilience in following through and taking risks, there are also some important differences. Female social entrepreneurs tend to be strongly motivated by social justice and often focus on women, youth, and children. This trend is consistent in social bricoleurs, social constructionists, and social engineers.

Social capital is important in social entrepreneurship, and research indicates that female social entrepreneurs tend to be more adept at social networking. In addition to networking, female social entrepreneurs also seem to be very good at multitasking and creating linkages among unlikely actors. They are less likely than men to set up a strong division between their public and private roles. Some of these qualities may also present challenges to women leaders, such as the potential for dissipation of energy resulting from over-networking and multitasking. In short, the case studies examined demonstrate that there are some specific motivational factors and explanations for success that are gender specific and invite further research in this area to add to our knowledge of how women social entrepreneurs are contributing to overall social change.

ACKNOWLEDGMENT

The authors wish to thank Ronit Yitshaki, from Bar Ilon University and Ariel University, for her contributions to this chapter.

REFERENCES

Acumen Fund. (n.d.). About Us. Retrieved from Acumen Fund website: http://www.acumenfund.org/about-us.html

Alvarez, S. (2000). Translating the global effects of transnational organizing in local feminist discourses and practices in Latin America. *Meridians: Feminism, Race, Transnationalism, 1*, 29–67.

Bornstein, D. (2007). *How to change the world: Social entrepreneurs and the power of new ideas* (updated ed.). New York, NY: Oxford University Press.

Carsud, A., & Brannback, M. (2011). Entrepreneurial motivations: What do we still need to know? *Journal of Small Business Management, 49*(10), 9–26.

Chhabra, E. (2011, July 1). Solar Sister wants to light up rural Africa. *Christian Science Monitor.* Retrieved from http://www.csmonitor.com/World/Making-a-difference/Change-Agent/2011/0701/Solar-Sister-wants-to-light-up-rural-Africa

Dees, J. G. (2001). *The meaning of "social entrepreneurship."* Duke University, Fuqua School of Business, Center for Advancement of Social Entrepreneurship, Durham, NC. Retrieved from http://www.caseatduke.org/documents/dees_sedef.pdf

De Mello e Souza, C. (2008). Grassroots leadership in the Network of Healthy Communities in Rio de Janeiro, Brazil: A gender perspective. *Gender & Development, 16*(3), 481–494.

Di Domenico, M., Haugh, H., & Tracey, P. (2010). Social bricolage: Theorizing social value creation in social enterprises. *Entrepreneurship, Theory and Practice, 34,* 681–703.

Haugh, H. (2005). A research agenda for social entrepreneurship. *Social Enterprise Journal, 1*(2), 1–12.

Hayek, F.A. (1945). *The use of knowledge in society.* American Economic Review, 35, 519-530.

Kardam, N. (2004). The emerging global gender equality regime from neoliberal and constructivist perspectives in international relations. *International Feminist Journal of Politics*, 6(1), 85–109.

Kelley, D. J., Brush, C. G., Greene, P. G., & Litovsky, Y. (2011). *Global entrepreneurship monitor, 2010 report: Women entrepreneurs worldwide.* Wellesley, MA: Babson College.

Kelley, D. J., Singer, S., & Herrington, M. (2012). *Global entrepreneurship monitor: 2011 global report.* Wellesley, MA: Babson College.

Kirzner, I. (1973). *Competition and entrepreneurship.* The University of Chicago Press, Chicago.

Kron, J. (2012, October 10). Women entrepreneurs drive growth in Africa. *New York Times.* Retrieved from http://www.nytimes.com/2012/10/11/world/africa/women-entrepreneurs-drive-growth-in-africa.html?pagewanted=al

Kropp, F., Lindsay, N. J., & Hancock, G. (2011). Cultural context as a moderator of private entrepreneurship investment behavior. In K. Hindle & K. Klyver (Eds.), *Handbook of research on new venture creation* (pp. 253–279). Cheltenham, UK: Edward Elgar.

Kropp, F., Lindsay, N. J., & Shoham, A. (2006). Entrepreneurial, market, and learning orientations and international entrepreneurial business venture performance in South Africa. *International Marketing Review, 23*(5), 504–523.

Levi-Strauss, C. (1967). *The savage mind.* Chicago, IL: University of Chicago Press.

Light, P. C. (2008). *The search for social entrepreneurship.* Washington, DC: Brookings Institution Press.

Lumpkin, G. T, & Dess, G. G. (1996). Clarifying the entrepreneurial construct and linking it to performance. *Academy of Management Review, 21*(1), 135–172.

Martin, R. L., & Osberg, S. (2007). Social entrepreneurship: The case for definition. *Stanford Social Innovation Review,*(10), 26-39.

Rauch, A., & Frese, M. (2007). Let's put the person back into entrepreneurship research: A meta-analysis on the relationship between business owners' personality traits, business creation and success. *European Journal of Work & Organizational Psychology, 16*(4), 353–385.

Reverso. (n.d.). Retrieved September 3, 2012, from dictionary.reverso.net/french-english/bricoleurs

Roper, J., & Cheney. G. (2005). Leadership, learning and human resource management: The meaning of social entrepreneurship today. *Corporate Government, 5*(3), 95–104.

Schumpeter, J. A. (1934). *The theory of economic development.* Oxford, England: Oxford University Press.

Schumpeter, J.A. (1942). *Capitalism, socialism and democracy.* Harper and Brothers, New York.

Seelos, C., & Mair, J. (2005). Social entrepreneurship: Creating new business models to serve the poor. *Business Horizons, 48,* 241–246.

Shaw, E., & Carter, S. (2007). Social entrepreneurship: Theoretical antecedents and empirical analysis of entrepreneurial processes and outcomes. *Journal of Small Business and Enterprise Development, 14*(3), 418–434.

Sullivan Mort, G., Weerawardena, J., & Carnegie, K. (2003). Social entrepreneurship: Toward conceptualization. *International Journal of Nonprofit and Voluntary Sector Marketing, 8*(1), 76–88.

Terjesen, S., Lepoutre, J., Justo, R., & Bosma, N. (2011). *Global entrepreneurship monitor report on social entrepreneurship executive summary.* Wellesley, MA: Babson College.

Yitshaki, R., & Kropp, F. (2011). Becoming a social entrepreneurs: Understanding motivations using a life story analysis. *International Journal of Business and Globalisation, 7*(3), 319–331.

Young, O. (1991). Political leadership and regime formation. *International Organization, 45,* 281–308.

Zahra, S. A., Gedajlovic, E., Neubaum, D. E., & Shulman, J. E. (2009). A typology of social entrepreneurs: Motives, search processes and ethical challenges. *Journal of Business Venturing, 24*, 519–532.

Chapter Three

WOMEN IN THE INFORMAL ECONOMY: ECONOMIC ACTORS AND GLOBAL LEADERS

MARTHA ALTER CHEN,
HARVARD KENNEDY SCHOOL

In the global economy today, across most developing countries, the majority of all workers—and a significant majority of women workers—are informally employed (Vanek, Chen, Hussmanns, Heintz, & Carre, 2012). And in developed countries, increasing numbers of once-formal workers are now informally employed: as part-time, temporary, contracted, and subcontracted workers or as self-employed. This global informal workforce contributes to national economies and is linked to the global economy through outsourced production and global supply chains, export-oriented production, and other backward and forward linkages. Yet too little is known about the global informal workforce, much less the women workers in it, and how it is incorporated into the global economy. Even less is known about how informal workers, especially women workers, organize to address the risks and seize the opportunities associated with the global economy.

This chapter seeks to fill this gap in knowledge and understanding. The first section briefly defines the informal economy and presents recent estimates of its size and composition. The second section disaggregates the recent data by sex, describes gender segmentation and wage gaps within the informal economy, and discusses why women are such important economic actors in the informal economy and the global economy. Section 3 describes a growing global alliance of organizations of informal workers, largely led by women leaders and women's organizations. The chapter concludes in Section 4 by asserting that the future of the global economy depends on the work of informal workers, especially women, and that the future of the international labor movement depends on joining hands with the growing movement of informal worker organizations and the women's organizations and women leaders within it.

The Informal Economy

What Is the Informal Economy?

Historically, the informal economy was widely seen as comprising self-employed persons engaged in informal activities and informal enterprises—with relatively little attention paid to wage workers employed under informal employment relationships. But over the past decade, the International Labour Organization (ILO), the international Expert Group on Informal Sector Statistics (called the Delhi Group), and the global network Women in Informal Employment: Globalizing and Organizing (WIEGO) have worked together to promote a broader concept and definition that incorporates certain types of informal employment, especially of women workers, that were not included in the earlier enterprise-based concept and definition. They sought to include the whole of work-related informality, as it is manifested in industrialized, transitional, and developing economies and the real-world dynamics in labor markets today, particularly the employment arrangements of the working poor, and especially women. Much of the impetus for broadening the definition came from the Self-Employed Women's Association (SEWA) of India whose membership—more than 1.3 million—is composed entirely of women informal workers, and whose leaders have long understood that data, in the hands of women workers, have power but that existing labor force data underestimate the numbers and types of women informal workers.

The expanded definition focuses on the nature of employment in addition to the characteristics of enterprises and includes all types of informal employment both inside and outside informal enterprises. It includes, for instance, paid domestic work in households and industrial outwork for formal firms—much of which is done by women. This expanded definition was endorsed by the International Labour Conference (ILC) in 2002 and the International Conference of Labour Statisticians (ICLS) in 2003. Earlier, in 1993, the ICLS had adopted an international statistical definition of the "informal sector" to refer to employment and production that takes place in unincorporated small and/or unregistered enterprises (ILO, 1993). In 2003, the ICLS broadened the definition to include the various types of informal employment outside informal enterprises, referring to this expanded notion as "informal employment" (ILO, 2003).

Informal employment, so defined, is a large and heterogeneous category. For purposes of analysis and policymaking, it is useful, first, to subdivide informal employment into self-employment and wage employment, and then within these broad categories, into more homogeneous subcategories according to status in employment, as follows:

Informal self-employment including:

- Employers in informal enterprises
- Own-account workers in informal enterprises
- Contributing family workers (in informal and formal enterprises)
- Members of informal producers' cooperatives (where these exist)

Informal wage employment: Employees hired without social protection contributions by formal or informal enterprises or as paid domestic workers by households. Certain types of wage work are more likely than others to be informal, including:

- Employees of informal enterprises
- Casual or day laborers
- Temporary or part-time workers
- Paid domestic workers
- Contract workers
- Unregistered or undeclared workers
- Industrial outworkers (also called homeworkers)

This expanded definition extends the focus from *enterprises* that are not legally regulated to include *employment relationships* that are not legally regulated or socially protected. It also serves to focus attention on informal workers, that is, those who are informally employed. This employment-centered focus has been accompanied by significant rethinking of the composition, causes, and consequences of informal employment. Today, informal employment is widely recognized to include a range of *self-employed* persons, who mainly work in unincorporated small or unregistered enterprises, as well as a range of *wage workers* who are employed by informal enterprises, formal enterprises, and households without employer contributions to social protection.

To sum up, there are three related official statistical terms and definitions that are often used imprecisely and interchangeably: The *informal sector* refers to the production and employment that takes place in unincorporated small or unregistered enterprises (1993 ICLS); *informal employment* refers to employment without legal and social protection—both inside and outside the informal sector (2003 ICLS); and the *informal economy* refers to all units, activities, and workers so defined and the output from them. Together, they form the broad base of the workforce and economy, both nationally and globally.

Why Is the Informal Economy Important?

Size and Significance

Since the expanded definition of "informal employment" was adopted by the 2002 ILC and the 2003 ICLS, more and more countries have begun using this definition of informal employment in the collection and tabulation of national labor force data.[1]

However, the data now available *internationally* are often limited to informal nonagricultural employment. This is because additional methodological work is required to apply the definition of informal employment to agriculture. What follows is a summary of recent analyses of available data on the size or significance of nonagricultural informal employment.

Informal employment represents a significant share of nonagricultural employment in developing regions, ranging from 51 percent in Latin America to 65 percent in East and Southeast Asia to 66 percent in sub-Saharan Africa (including South Africa and other countries in Southern Africa with a relatively low prevalence of informal employment) to 82 percent in South Asia. Informal employment represents 10 percent of nonagricultural employment in Eastern Europe and Central Asia (Vanek, Chen, Hussmanns, Heintz, et al., 2012).

There is significant variation by country within the regions, from 40 percent (Uruguay) to 75 percent (Bolivia) in Latin America; from 33 percent (urban China) to 42 percent (Thailand) to 73 percent (Indonesia) in East and Southeast Asia; from 33 percent (South Africa) to 82 percent (Mali) in sub-Saharan Africa; from 62 percent (Sri Lanka) to 83 percent (India) in South Asia. In those countries and regions where agriculture still employs a large share of the workforce, the share of total informal employment in total employment is likely to be higher still (ILO, 2002).[2] In some countries in Africa and South Asia that measure informal employment in agriculture, informal employment represents 90 percent or more of total employment: notably, Ghana and India (ILO, 2002).

Links with Poverty and Growth

Not all informal workers are poor, and not all working poor are engaged in the informal economy. Some informal operators—especially among those who hire others—are not poor, and some formal wage workers are poor. But there is a significant overlap between working in the informal economy and being poor. This is because, on average, earnings are lower and risks are higher in the informal economy compared to the formal economy.

Although the informal economy is associated with low productivity and low incomes, it nonetheless contributes to the economy. The informal economy produces high-end goods and services used in the formal economy as well as low-cost goods and services consumed by the poor and middle class. Recent estimates indicate that the share of the informal sector (excluding agriculture) in nonagricultural gross value added (GVA) is significant, ranging from one-half of nonagricultural GVA in countries in west Africa to 46 percent in India to 29 percent in the Middle East and North Africa region, 25 percent in Latin America region, and 14 percent in the transition countries (Vanek, 2010).

But these estimates do not include the contribution of the informal workforce outside the informal sector (i.e., outside informal enterprises). To precisely measure the contribution of the total informal economy to GVA will require better estimates of the contribution of informal enterprises as well as estimates of the contribution of informal workers outside informal enterprises: in formal firms, in global value chains, for households (i.e., domestic workers), in agriculture, and in secondary activities. Mexico is the only country that has estimates of the contribution of the *total* informal economy, inside and outside the informal sector. In Mexico, the total informal economy contributes just over 30 percent of total GVA. The contribution of informal employment outside the informal sector (17 percent) is greater than the contribution of the informal sector (13 percent) (special tabulations by the National Statistical Institute of Mexico cited in Vanek, Chen, & Hussmanns, 2012).[3] These estimates underscore the significant contribution that the informal economy makes to the economy of Mexico and the need to measure the contribution of both the informal sector and informal employment outside the informal sector.

Women in the Informal Economy

Significance of Women in the Informal Economy

In many regions, informal employment is a more important source of employment for women than for men. In sub-Saharan Africa, informal employment represents

74 percent of women's nonagricultural employment in contrast to 61 percent of men's; in Latin America and the Caribbean,[4] 54 percent in contrast to 48 percent; and in South Asia, 83 percent in contrast to 82 percent. In six cities in China, 36 percent of women workers in contrast to 30 percent of men workers are informally employed. However, it is important to highlight that in all regions and urban China, men represent the majority of the informal workforce because women's labor force participation rates are lower than men's.

Employment in the informal sector (i.e., within informal enterprises) often accounts for a larger share of men's nonagricultural employment than women's, the notable exception being sub- Saharan Africa and urban China. The opposite is true for informal employment outside the informal sector: The proportion for women is larger than for men, again with the exception of sub-Saharan Africa and urban China. This is because women tend to be disproportionately employed as informal domestic workers in households, industrial outworkers or informal employees for formal firms, and unpaid contributing family workers in formal firms.

Women in informal employment are more likely to be self-employed than are men, the clear exception being Eastern Europe and Central Asia, but also Latin America where roughly equal shares of women and men informal workers are self-employed. Within self-employment, women are far more likely than men to be unpaid contributing family workers in family enterprises and also more likely to be own-account workers who do not hire others. The exception, in regard to own-account work, is South Asia where own-account workers compose a larger proportion of men's nonagricultural informal employment than women's, although the reverse is true for self-employment as a whole. This is because unpaid contributing work accounts for a particularly large share of women's informal employment in South Asia.

Across all developing regions, services other than trade and transportation account for a larger share of women's, than men's, informal employment. Manufacturing accounts for an equal or greater share of women's, than men's, informal employment in all regions, except for sub-Saharan Africa. A similar pattern holds for trading activities, with the notable exception of the Middle East, North Africa, and South Asia: In both these regions, many communities discourage women from working outside their homes or engaging with strangers. Very few women work in informal construction and transportation activities—the one modest exception being South Asia where there are still large numbers of women construction workers. Agricultural self-employment accounts for a larger share of women's, than men's, informal employment, in East, South, and Southeast Asia and in sub-Saharan Africa.

Gender Segmentation and Wage Gaps within the Informal Economy

In the late 1990s, the WIEGO network commissioned two reviews of the links between informality, poverty, and gender: one of available literature (Sethuraman,

1998), the other of available statistics (Charmes, 1998). Both reviews found a similar hierarchy of earnings and segmentation by employment status and sex. These common findings provided the basis for the WIEGO multisegmented model illustrated in Figure 3.1.

In 2004, WIEGO commissioned data analysts to test this model in six developing countries—Costa Rica, Egypt, El Salvador, Ghana, India, and South Africa—by analyzing national data in those countries (Chen et al., 2005). Official national data for casual day laborers and industrial outworkers were not available in these countries. But the available data allowed for a comparison of employment status (measured at the individual level) and income poverty (measured at the household level), making it possible to estimate the percentage of workers in specific employment statuses who were from poor households (what WIEGO calls "poverty risk"). In all countries, average earnings went down and the risk of being from a poor household went up as workers moved down the employment statuses in the WIEGO model.

FIGURE 3.1: HIERARCHY OF EARNINGS AND POVERTY RISK BY EMPLOYMENT STATUS AND SEX

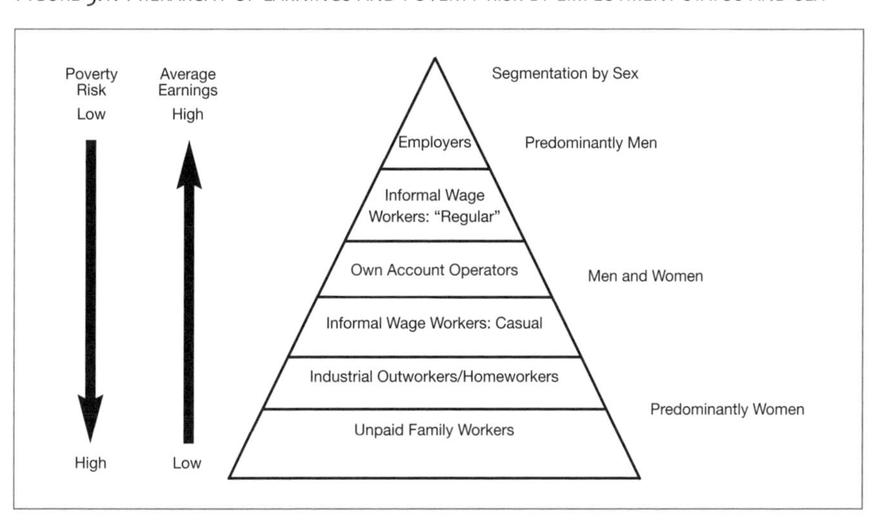

An additional fact, not captured in Figure 3.1, is that there is further segmentation of employment within these broad status categories. Women tend to be employed in different types of activities, associated with different levels of earning, than men—with the result that they tend to earn less even within specific segments of the informal economy. Some of this difference can be explained by the fact that men tend to have *better tools*, operate from *better work sites/spaces* and have *greater access to productive assets and financial capital*. In addition, or as a result, men often produce or sell a *higher volume* or a *different range* of goods and services. For instance, among street vendors in some countries, men are more likely to sell nonperishable goods, while women are more likely to sell perishable goods (such as fruits and vegetables). In addition, men are more likely to sell from pushcarts or bicycles, while women are more likely to sell from baskets on their heads or on the ground, or simply from a cloth spread on the ground. This is also because men are more likely to be heads of family businesses, while women are more likely to be unpaid contributing family members (Chen, Vanek, & Carr, 2004).

Contributions of Women Informal Workers

As noted earlier, the informal workforce contributes to the economy. It produces high-end goods and services used by the formal economy as well as low-cost goods and services consumed by the poor and middle class. Women workers in the informal economy also contribute to the economies of their households by bringing in much-needed income and allocating most of it to the household budget. Many women informal workers are integrated into the global economy (Chen et al., 2004). Women domestic workers from the global South migrate to the global North to provide child care, elderly care, cooking, and cleaning services. The bottom link in most global supply chains is women producing goods from their homes under subcontracts to firms up the supply chain: producing goods ranging from garments, shoes, and soccer balls to electronic goods to parts for automobiles and airplanes. While macro data are not available on the informal economy in global supply chains, micro studies indicate that women home-based producers represent large percentages of the workforce in export-oriented production, especially in garments and textiles, footwear, and sporting goods (Chen, Carr, & Tate, 2000; Chen, Sebstad, & O'Connell, 1999). Women street vendors are key actors in the global distribution system, often selling imported goods to customers not reached by formal retailers. Women and men waste pickers around the world reclaim recyclable waste from households, dumpsters, streets, landfills, and other sites; sort, bundle, and compact the recyclable waste; and then sell the reclaimed waste to recycling depots that resell the waste to enterprises up the recycling chain (much of the reclaimed waste enters the global market for raw materials and packing materials controlled by very large multinational waste recycling firms).[5] In sum, women informal workers represent the real "bottom of the economic pyramid" contributing to their household economy, their country's economy, and the global economy.[6]

Women Leaders and Organizations[7] in the Informal Economy

Organizing of informal workers dates back to the beginning of the trade union movement when all workers were informal. It was only as unions got stronger that a "formal" workforce began to emerge, one in which workers enjoyed minimum wages, social protection, and other benefits negotiated through collective agreements or legislation (Gallin, 2011). But not all informal workers got formal wage jobs: Some remained self-employed, some remained in informal wage jobs, and others entered informal wage jobs. Most of them remained outside the formal trade unions. Over the years in different countries, groups of such workers began to organize themselves, including groups of women workers led by pioneering women leaders. Around 1900, seasonal workers (called *mondine*)—mostly women—in the rice fields of Northern Italy organized strikes to demand higher wages, shorter working hours, and housing. They won their first major victory—an eight-hour workday—in 1909. Although they affiliated with the agricultural workers' union, the *mondine* continued their own struggles for higher wages until rice cultivation was mechanized and herbicides were introduced beginning in the 1950s (Gallin). In 1927 in Bolivia, a group of women workers created the General Women Workers' Union (*Sindicato Feminino de Oficios Varios*), which "included cooks working in households, laundry workers, dairy workers, flower vendors and other street and market vendors. As membership grew, separate unions were established for the different categories of workers and the union was eventually reorganized as the Women Workers' Federation (Federación Obrera Feminina (FOF)" (Gallin, p. 4).

The Self-Employed Women's Association (SEWA)

Recent organizing of informal workers dates back to the founding, in 1972, of the Self-Employed Women's Association (SEWA), a multisector trade union of women informal workers in India. The seeds of SEWA were planted in 1920, when inspired by Mahatma Gandhi, Ansooya-ben Sarabhai (the daughter of a textile mill owner) started a union of textile workers called the Textile Labour Association (TLA) in Ahmedabad City, in western India. For the next 60 years, the textile industry—including the TLA and its institutional counterpart, the Ahmedabad Mill Owners Association—dominated the economic and political landscape of Ahmedabad City. In 1955, a young woman lawyer named Ela Bhatt joined the TLA. In 1968, after working for more than a decade on labor issues, Bhatt was asked to head the Women's Wing of the TLA.

The mandate of the Women's Wing was to provide training and welfare services to the wives of textile mill workers. But in 1971, a small group of migrant women cart pullers in the wholesale cloth market of Ahmedabad approached the Women's Wing to ask whether the TLA might be able to help them find housing. Ela Bhatt accompanied the women to the wholesale cloth market, where she met another group of women who were working as head loaders and carrying loads of cloth to and from the wholesale market. The head loaders described their work, including their low and erratic wages. The head loaders were paid on a per-trip basis by the merchants—not according to the distance traveled or weight carried. Because no records were maintained of how many trips they made, they were often not paid the full amount they were owed.

Under the auspices of the Women's Wing of the TLA, Ela Bhatt decided to organize a public meeting for the head loaders in the cloth market to discuss their problems. During the meeting, she told the women that they should organize if they wished to address their problems. The women agreed to organize themselves into a group and each paid 25 *paisa* (quarter of a rupee) as a membership fee. Following the meeting, Ela Bhatt wrote an article for a local newspaper detailing the problems of the head loaders. The cloth merchants countered with their own news story in which they denied the allegations and claimed that they treated the head loaders fairly. The Women's Wing responded by reprinting the merchant's claims of fair treatment on cards that they distributed to the head loaders to use to hold the merchants accountable, thus turning the merchant's rebuttal to the head loaders' advantage (Sebstad, 1982).

Word of the head loaders' moral victory spread quickly. Soon, a group of used-clothing dealers approached the TLA Women's Wing with their complaints. Again, Ela Bhatt called a public meeting to which over 100 used-garment dealers and other women came. During that meeting, a woman from the crowd suggested they form an association of their own. Thus, on an appeal from women workers in the informal economy and at the initiative of a woman lawyer and the TLA Women's Wing, SEWA was born on December 3, 1971. The rest, as the saying goes, is SEWA's history.[8] Today SEWA has more than 1.3 million members—all working poor women in the informal economy—in 10 states across India. Also today, SEWA is a lead organization in a growing global alliance of the working poor, especially women, in the informal economy.

Since its official founding in 1972, when it was registered as a trade union, SEWA has pursued a joint strategy of what it calls "struggle" and "development." As a workers union, SEWA represents the interests of its members and undertakes struggles for their rights. At the same time, SEWA has promoted a variety of member-based SEWA organizations, mainly cooperatives, which contribute to various aspects of development bringing the SEWA members into the economic and social mainstream. Today, more than 100 SEWA organizations constitute a sisterhood of institutions owned and managed by SEWA members, the women workers of the informal economy. As a trade union, SEWA undertakes the following activities, tailored to members' main occupation or trade:

Organization: into trade groups or cooperatives or producer groups

Local leadership development: opportunities and training to become local leaders

Collective bargaining: trade-wise or issue-based

Policy advocacy: trade-wise or issue-based

All members of SEWA belong to a relevant trade group and are voting members of the SEWA union; many also belong to one or more other membership-based organizations—cooperatives, producer groups, and (in rural areas) savings-and-credit groups and producer companies. All these enterprises are run co-operatively with shares owned by SEWA members who elect their own boards. The developmental activities of the SEWA sister organizations include:

Financial services: savings, loans, insurance and pensions

Social protection: health, child care, and education (adult literacy)

Infrastructure services: housing plus water, sanitation, electricity, and (in remote areas) transportation

Capacity-building services: training in technical skills, leadership, and other skills

Business development services: skills training and product development

Marketing services: local, state, national, and export marketing services

Clearly, not all organizations of informal workers can or should aspire to this full range of interventions. But the SEWA example illustrates what is needed to overcome the negative policy and regulatory environment faced by informal workers and to provide the supportive services that informal workers, especially women, need—and typically do not receive—to make their work more remunerative and secure.

Other Organizations of Informal Workers

During the 1980s and 1990s, a significant number of organizations of informal workers were formed, including local and national cooperatives or associations of waste pickers in Argentina, Brazil, Colombia, Ecuador, and India; national associations of home-based workers in Bangladesh, Philippines, and Thailand; national associations of street vendors in many countries; a regional alliance of home-based workers in Southeast Asia; and a regional confederation of domestic workers in Latin American and the Caribbean.

Working with trade unions and NGOs (nongovernmental organizations), SEWA helped to establish linkages between organizations of home-based workers and street vendors. This led to the founding of two international networks: one of women home-based workers called HomeNet, and the other of women and men street vendors called StreetNet International. At the first meeting of HomeNet in 1994, the founding members planned a global campaign for an international convention that would recognize and protect home-based workers. The campaign proved successful: In June 1996, the ILC voted in in favor of an international convention on homework (C177). HomeNet continued to work closely with HomeNet

Southeast Asia and other organizations of home-based workers and to jointly advocate for national policies to support them, including ratification of the Homework Convention. The international HomeNet was dissolved in 2000 due to differences over its constitution and structure, but a second regional network, HomeNet South Asia, was formed that year. Today, the two regional HomeNets—South and Southeast Asia—have a combined total of 11 national associations of home-based workers allied with them.

At the first international meeting on street vendors convened by SEWA in Bellagio, Italy, in 1995, a group of activists from 11 countries adopted an International Declaration that set forth a plan to promote local and national policies to support and protect the rights of street vendors. For the next several years, they organized regional meetings of street vendors in Asia, Africa, and Latin America and provided support to newly emerging local and national associations of street vendors in several countries. This led to the formation of StreetNet International in November 2002. StreetNet International held its first International Congress in March 2004, attended by 58 delegates from 15 organizations, at which an international council was elected for a three-year term. StreetNet International today has over 500, 000 dues-paying street vendor members in 48 affiliates in 40 countries.

During the final year of the campaign for the homework convention, SEWA and HomeNet commissioned a researcher at Harvard University (this author) to compile available statistics on homework for dissemination at the 1996 ILO annual conference (Chen et al., 1999) and requested the United National Development Fund for Women (UNIFEM) to convene a policy dialogue in Asia with government delegations to the June 1996 ILC. These initiatives contributed to the successful campaign for the ILO Convention on Homework (C177).

Recognizing the power of the joint action of organizations of informal workers, researcher institutions, and international development agencies, SEWA, UNIFEM, and this author organized a meeting of 10 experts on the informal economy—including representatives from HomeNet, researchers and statisticians from academic institutions and international agencies, and development professionals from the ILO and the World Bank—at Bellagio in 1997. The experts decided to establish a global action-research-policy network to promote better statistics, research, programs, and policies in support of women in the informal economy, and they named the network Women in Informal Employment: Globalizing and Organizing (WIEGO).

Since 1997, the WIEGO network has joined hands with SEWA, other trade unions and organizations of informal workers, and NGOs to help build and strengthen national networks of home-based workers and street vendors, which are the regional HomeNets in South and Southeast Asia, and the global network StreetNet International. Together they have also helped build or strengthen national, regional, and international networks of two other groups of informal workers:

domestic workers and waste pickers. Together they have highlighted that being organized into membership-based organizations (MBOs) enables the working poor, especially women, to gain representative voice and effectively made demands; bargain collectively; and negotiate supportive policies, programs, and practice.[9] And together they are committed to promoting women members and leaders within the organizations of the working poor in the informal economy.

The organizations of domestic workers and home-based workers have primarily women members and leaders, while the organizations of street vendors and waste pickers have both men and women members and, to date, primarily men leaders. This reflects gender dynamics within the organizations but also the reality of these occupations on the ground: The vast majority of domestic workers and home-based workers around the world are women, whereas the ratio of men to women in street vending and waste picking depends, respectively, on social norms and the income level of countries. In societies that restrict the physical mobility of women, there are fewer women street vendors. In higher-income countries where waste management has been modernized for a longer time, there tend to be fewer women waste pickers; the reverse is true in lower-income countries where waste management has not yet been modernized. For instance, more waste pickers are women in Central America, Bolivia, and Ecuador than elsewhere in Latin America.[10]

StreetNet International, which is led by a woman trade unionist from South Africa, is committed to ensuring that half of the members of its international council and half of the leaders of its affiliate organizations are women. Inspired by the HomeNets, SEWA, and StreetNet International, the associations of waste pickers have begun to explore the gender dynamics within their membership and leadership. A related point is that most of the organizations of street vendors and waste pickers were started by the informal workers themselves, while most of the organizations of domestic workers and home-based workers were formed with the help of, respectively, trade unions and nongovernmental organizations (NGOs). This difference is not surprising given that street vendors and waste pickers, who work in open public space, have opportunities to meet and to self-organize while home-based workers and domestic workers, who work in private homes, do not.

Since 2000, there has been a steady increase in the numbers and geographic scope of organizations of informal workers, including: the formation of national associations of waste pickers in several Latin American countries (Bolivia, Brazil, Chile, Ecuador, Nicaragua, Peru, Uruguay, and Venezuela); a Latin America regional alliance of waste pickers; a national association of waste pickers in South Africa; national associations of domestic workers in South Africa and the United States; a regional network of home-based workers in South Asia; and global alliances and networks of domestic workers (the International Domestic Workers Network) and of waste pickers (the Global Alliance of Waste Pickers).

Soon after its founding in 2008, the International Domestic Workers Network mounted a campaign for an international convention on domestic work. In June 2011, the ILC approved with a significant majority vote an international convention on Decent Work for Domestic Workers (C189). The fact that a delegation of domestic workers (all women except for one man from Benin) participated in the two ILCs (in 2010 and 2011) when the convention was discussed—articulating their demands very forcefully and effectively—contributed to the successful outcome of the campaign. The International Union of Food and Allied Workers and the WIEGO network provided joint support to the formation of the International Domestic Workers Network and its campaign for the convention. For more details, see Bonner and Spooner (2011).

At the local level, organizing of informal workers takes different forms: from trade unions to cooperatives to associations of various kinds to savings-and-credit groups or self-help groups.

In large part, the local political and legal environment shapes organizational forms. For instance, in many countries, there are unregistered associations that function like cooperatives or trade unions but find it difficult to register as a cooperative or trade union. But in some part, organizational form follows organizational function. Domestic workers who need solidarity in order to bargain with their employers often form or join trade unions. Self-employed, home-based workers often form associations or small producer groups to leverage skills training, product design, and marketing services. But industrial outworkers who work from their home need to form unions—or borrow union tactics—for collective bargaining with employers and their intermediaries. Street vendors who need to bargain collectively with local authorities often form unions or market-specific associations. Waste pickers who provide recycling services to cities or cleaning services to firms often form cooperatives.

As noted earlier, most of the national, regional, and international alliances or networks are formed along sector lines (domestic workers, home-based workers, street vendors, and waste pickers). But within these sector-based networks are workers with different statuses in employment (both self-employed and dependent workers) and organizations of different forms (unions, cooperatives, associations). Some of the networks include both organizations of informal workers and NGOs that support them. Most of the networks seek to enhance the representative voice and official visibility of informal workers and to build and strengthen the collective bargaining and advocacy of their affiliates.

Many of these organizations and networks collaborate on joint projects or advocacy efforts. An alliance of these organizations was instrumental in establishing the Conclusions to the General Discussion on Decent Work and the Informal Economy at the ILC in 2002. It did so by writing technical papers on the informal economy for the ILO, organizing regional workshops of organizations working in the informal economy to draft a common platform of demands and convening a coalition of delegates and observers at the conference. A consortium of the two regional HomeNets, SEWA, StreetNet International, several waste picker organizations, and the WIEGO network plus other support NGOs is engaged in a six-year, multiple-country project called Inclusive Cities for the Urban Working Poor. Launched in 2008, the Inclusive Cities project aims to strengthen MBOs of the working poor in the urban informal economy in the areas of organizing, policy analysis, and advocacy, in order to ensure that urban informal workers have the tools to effectively voice their demands and concerns within urban planning, rule setting, and policymaking processes (see www.inclusivecities.org). Two other consortia involving the regional HomeNets, HomeNet Thailand, the International Domestic Workers Network, StreetNet International, women's producer groups linked to the Fair Trade movement, *Asiye eTafuleni* (a South African support NGO), and the WIEGO network have been engaged in multiyear multicountry projects to build the economic power, leadership, and voice of women leaders and organizations in the informal economy.

Working together, these organizations are forging a growing global alliance of the working poor, especially women, in the informal economy. As described earlier, much of this effort has been led by women leaders and women's organizations in the informal economy, inspired by the pioneering vision and strategies of SEWA, and supported by the WIEGO network. There is little doubt that without SEWA, the other women leaders and women's organizations in the informal economy and the WIEGO network there would not be a growing global alliance today of the working poor, especially women, in the informal economy.

Moving Forward

Given the facts and figures presented here, a case can be made that the future of the global economy depends on the work and output of informal workers, especially women. Undoubtedly, the informal economy represents the broad base of economic units, actors, activities, and output in today's global economy. All indications are that the informal economy is here to stay, is growing in some contexts, and is appearing in new guises in both developed and developing countries.

Given the examples in this chapter, a case can also be made that the future of the international labor movement depends on joining hands with the growing movement of informal worker organizations and the women leaders and women's organizations within it. The sheer size of the global informal workforce requires solidarity between formal and informal workers. The organizing strategies and organizational forms developed by the members of the global alliance of informal workers point the direction for future organizing in the informal economy and across the informal—formal divide.

Certainly, a case can also be made that poverty and inequality cannot be reduced without increasing the incomes and reducing the risks of the working poor, especially women, in the informal economy. The world of work is the key pathway to reducing income poverty because their labor—their work—is the primary (often only) source of income for the poor. Most of the working poor, especially women, are engaged in the informal economy, and most of the informal workforce, especially women, is poor.

For these and other reasons, what is needed is vision of the informal economy that sees the working poor, especially women, as part of a global solution to increase growth and to decrease poverty and inequality. What is needed is a vision of the global economy that allows the informal economy to operative alongside the formal economy and promotes fair and equitable relationships between the two. Most critically, what are needed are more and stronger women leaders and women's organizations in the informal economy to continue to help leading the way to realizing this vision.

NOTES

[1] The ILO-WIEGO database on informal employment now contains data for nearly 50 countries: see http://www.ilo.org/global/statistics-and-databases/WCMS_179795/lang—en/index.htm

[2] This report was written by Martha Chen and Joann Vanek using multicountry data analyzed by Jacques Charmes; additional data analysis by Marge Guerrero; country studies by Debbie Budlender, Peter Buwembo, and Nozipho Shabala (South Africa), Rodrigo Negrete (Mexico), and Jeemol Unni (India); and analysis of developed country data by Françoise Carré, and Joaquin Herranz, Jr.

[3] Both the data and the text on Mexico were prepared by Rodrigo Negrete and Guadalupe Luna of the research unit with the support of Tomas Ramirez, Mario Moreno, and Efrain Munoz from the Labour Force Unit of the Instituto Nacional de Estadistica, Geografia e Informatica (INEGI), Mexico.

[4] No direct estimates of informal employment were available for the Caribbean countries; however, indirect estimates were included for some of the countries of the subregion.

[5] For more details, see http://wiego.org/informal-economy/occupational-groups

[6] An indicator of how closely women informal workers are integrated into the global economy is the fact that waste pickers and home-based workers who reclaim recyclable waste and produce goods, respectively, for the global economy felt the impact as early as October–November 2008 from the global financial crisis that started in September 2008. Knowing this impact was being felt, the global network WIEGO with its partners in the Inclusive Cities project carried out two rounds of a 10-city study on the impact of, first, the crisis and, then, the lingering recession (in mid-2001 and again in mid-2010): see Horn (2009) and Chen (2012) for analyses of the research findings.

[7] While there are several books and multiple articles on the Self-Employed Women's Association (SEWA) in India (see footnote 8), documentation and analysis of the other organizations is less readily available. This section draws on the experience of the WIEGO network and its members (Chen, 2000) as well as recent documentation and analysis commissioned by WIEGO, including a database (the WORD database) of over 600 organizations; an analysis of that database (Miller, 2012); an annotated bibliography of organizing in the informal economy (Vainio, 2012); and two recent articles (Bonner & Spooner, 2011; Mather, 2012). The reader should refer to these publications for more details, including the names and descriptions of specific organizations.

[8] The summary above is based on a case study by this author (Chen 2008), which draws on three books on SEWA. The most recent book on SEWA was written by its founder, Ela Bhatt (Bhatt, 2006). Two earlier books on SEWA were written by Jennefer Sebstad (1982) and Kalima Rose (1992).

[9] See Chen, Jhabvala, Kanbur, and Richards (2007), an edited volume on membership-based organizations of the poor, for a set of case studies that illustrate that the poor need and can build their own organizations in order to shape and hold accountable the policy and regulatory environment that affects their lives and work.

[10] L. Fernandez, WIEGO Global Coordinator for Waste Picking (personal communication, September 2012).

REFERENCES

Bhatt, E. (2006). *We are poor, but so many.* New York, NY: Oxford University Press.

Bonner, C., & Spooner, D. (2011, January). Organizing labour in the informal economy: Institutional forms & relationships. *Labour, Capital and Society, 44*(1). http://wiego.org/sites/wiego.org/files/publications/files/Bonner_Spooner_Organizing_Labour.pdf

Charmes, J. (1998). *Informal sector, poverty and gender: A review of empirical evidence.* Geneva, Switzerland: World Bank.

Chen, M. A. (2000). Women in the informal sector: A global picture, the global movement. *SAIS Review, 21*(1), 71–82.

Chen, M. A.. (2008). A spreading banyan tree: The self-employed women's association, India. In A. Mathie & G. Cunningham (Eds.), *From clients to citizens: Communities changing the course of their own development* (pp. 181–206). Rugby, UK: Intermediate Technology.

Chen, M. A.. (2012). Global recession and the informal economy: Evidence from Latin America and beyond. In M. Cohen (Ed.), *The global economic crisis in Latin America* (pp. 115–136). New York, NY: Routledge Press.

Chen, M., Carr, M., & Tate, J. (2000). Globalization and home-based workers. *Feminist Economics, 6*(3), 123–142.

Chen, M., Jhabvala, R., Kanbur, R., & Richards, C. (Eds.). (2007). *Member-based organizations of the poor: Concepts, experience, and policy.* New York, NY: Routledge Press.

Chen, M., Sebstad, J., & O'Connell, L. (1999). Counting the invisible workforce: The case of home-based workers. *World Development, 27*(3), 603–610.

Chen, M., Vanek, J., & Carr, M. (2004). *Mainstreaming informal employment and gender in poverty reduction: A handbook for policymakers and other stakeholders.* London, UK: Commonwealth Secretariat.

Chen, M., Vanek, J., Lund, F., Heintz, J., Jhabvala, R., & Bonner, C. (2005). *Progress of the world's women 2005: Women, work and poverty.* New York, NY: UNIFEM.

Gallin, D. (2011, March). *Organizing informal workers: Historical overview.* Speech at WIEGO Workshop on Organizing Informal Workers: Building & Strengthening Membership-Based Organizations held in Bangkok, Thailand. Retrieved from http://wiego.org/informal-economy/occupational-groups

Horn, Z. E. (2009). *No cushion to fall back on: The global economic crisis and informal workers.* Cambridge, MA: WIEGO and Inclusive Cities.

Horn, Z. E. (2011). *Coping with crises: Lingering recession, rising inflation, and the informal workforce.* Cambridge, MA: WIEGO and Inclusive Cities.

International Labour Organization (ILO). (1993). *Report of the Fifteenth International Conference of Labour Statisticians.* Geneva, Switzerland: ILO.

International Labour Organization (ILO). (2002). *Women and men in the informal economy: A statistical picture.* Geneva, Switzerland: Author.

International Labour Organization (ILO). (2003). *Report of the Seventeenth International Conference of Labour Statisticians.* Geneva, Switzerland: ILO.

Mather, C. (2012, February). *Informal workers' organizing* (WIEGO Publication Series). Retrieved from http://wiego.org/sites/wiego.org/files/publications/files/mather_informal_workers_organizing.pdf

Miller, S. (2012). *Analysis of the WIEGO Organization and Representation Data-Base (WORD)* (Report prepared for WIEGO). Cambridge, MA: WIEGO. Retrieved from http://wiego.org/sites/wiego.org/files/resources/files/Miller_WIEGO-WORD-Analysis-Report.pdf

Rose, K. (1992). *Where women are leaders: The SEWA movement in India.* New Delhi, India: Vistaar.

Sebstad, J. (1982). *Struggle and development among self-employed women: A report on the Self-Employed Women's Association, Ahmedabad.* Washington, DC: USAID.

Sethuraman, S. V. (1998). *Gender, informality and poverty: A global review.* Geneva, Switzerland: World Bank.

Vainio, A. (2012). *Annotated bibliography on organizing informal workers* (Report prepared for WIEGO). Cambridge, MA: WIEGO. Retrieved from http://wiego.org/sites/wiego.org/files/resources/files/WIEGO-Annotated-Bibliography-on_Organizing_Informal_Workers.pdf

Vanek, J. (2010). Improving statistics on informal employment in India: The role of users. In United Nations, *The World's Women 2010: Trends and statistics* (p. 90).

Vanek, J., Chen, M., & Hussmanns, R.. (2012). *Statistics on the informal economy: Definitions, findings, and challenges* (WIEGO Working Paper No. 2). Cambridge, MA: WIEGO.

Vanek, J., Chen, M., Hussmanns, R., Heintz, J., & Carre, F. (2012). *Women and men in the informal economy: A statistical picture.* Geneva, Switzerland: ILO and WIEGO.

Chapter Four

Bridging the Technology Gender Divide

Ann Mei Chang, Senior Advisor for Women and Technology, Secretary's Office of Global Women's Issues, U.S. Department of State

Information and communication technology (ICT), particularly mobile phones and the Internet, has been a transformative force in the modern world. With more than six billion subscriptions worldwide, mobile phones are starting to approach ubiquity. Meanwhile, the Internet, with over two billion users worldwide, is also approaching ubiquity in high-income countries, with usage by over 70 percent of the population. Still, in most low- to medium-income countries, while the Internet is a fast-growing phenomenon, it largely remains a tool for the wealthier and more educated segments of society, with an average of 26 percent of the population connected, dropping to only 13 percent on the African continent (International Telecommunication Union [ITU], 2012).

Technology as a Driver for Economic Growth

ICT holds tremendous potential as a tool for economic growth and human development. ICT increases productivity and efficiency of businesses both big and small, opens new markets within the country and abroad, and creates high quality jobs in the technology sector. ICT can also improve access to education and healthcare, increase civic engagement, and drive new innovations that fundamentally transform the way people interact and do business. Over the past five years, in developed countries, the Internet has accounted for an average of 3.4 percent of the overall GDP and 21 percent of the GDP growth (du Rausas et al., 2011). Increasing access to, usage of, and jobs within ICT can have multiplicative effects through the economy.

As mobile phones and the Internet become essential tools in both personal and professional lives, access to and use of these technologies will be an increasingly critical factor in women's ability to contribute fully to their individual, familial, and societal outcomes. Along with access to markets, finance, and education, increasing access to ICT by removing gender-related barriers is necessary to fully realize the potential economic contribution of women. ICT can also be an effective tool for delivery of relevant information and services to improve women's lives, exemplified by the dramatic impact on productivity and financial inclusion brought about by Mobile Money. And, the ICT sector itself presents a growing opportunity for well-paying jobs and professional careers, one that may also offer the flexibility to accommodate the competing demands women face in their lives.

In our modern, connected world, ICT has become increasingly the means with which people learn, become informed about the world around them, connect with friends and opportunities, and give themselves a voice. By fully capitalizing on possibilities of ICT, we can enable women to achieve a greater degree of personal empowerment, reduce isolation, increase their capabilities, combat stereotypes, and ultimately affirm their inherent human dignity.

Access to Technology

A seminal study published by the GSMA (Groupe Speciale Mobile Association) Development Fund and the Cherie Blair Foundation for Women (2010) found that a woman is 21 percent less likely to own a mobile phone than a man in low- and middle-income countries. The study spawned the GSMA mWomen Program, which aims to halve the mobile gender gap that accounts for 300 million women by bringing together major telecommunication companies and technology firms, donor agencies such as the U.S. Agency for International Development (USAID) and the Australian Agency for International Development (AusAID), financial institutions including Visa, and a wide range of players across civil society and industry. At the October 2010 launch of mWomen, former U.S. Secretary of State Hillary Rodham Clinton stated, "Investing in women is an investment in families, communities, and countries. Investing in women's progress is the most direct and effective way to invest in progress economically and socially globally."

While there has not yet been a similarly comprehensive study on Internet usage and gender, several sources indicate that when it comes to the Internet, the gender gap may be almost twice the size of the mobile gender gap. A 2008 International Telecommunication Union (ITU) report found that more than twice as many men as women were accessing the Internet in several African countries (ITU, 2011, Table 5.3). And, on perhaps the most widely used Internet service, Facebook, there are approximately 40 percent fewer female than male users in Africa, in contrast to slightly more female users in most developed countries.

This dramatic difference in access to such key technologies results in fewer opportunities for women to reach their full potential and a loss of significant economic and social contributions to their families and communities. Without a mobile phone, a woman may need to travel long distances, at considerable time and risk, to check on market prices or make financial transactions. She may not be able to obtain healthcare advice or call a doctor in times of crisis. And, without the Internet, her access to information to further her own and her children's education, obtain practical tools for her business, or engage with the government and civil society will be limited.

So, what has caused this gender gap in access to mobile phones and the Internet? Most of the barriers that prevent women in the developing world from accessing the Internet exist for men as well. Thus, solutions will reap benefits across the entire population, both directly and indirectly. However, these barriers often disproportionately impact women due to their more limited financial resources, educational training, or societal status. Women can also face additional barriers, particularly due to cultural expectations and norms that constrain their access to and use of technology. In developing countries, the most common challenges include the following:

Cultural barriers. In conservative and traditional societies, women are frequently discouraged from having a mobile phone or accessing the Internet by their fathers, husbands, or brothers, who may associate use of ICT with promiscuity. Other women may be uncomfortable or unable to interact with an unfamiliar male agent during the purchasing process. Visiting a cyber café can be socially awkward or even unsafe, as many are dominated by men. Such cultural norms stymie women at each step and make ownership both inconvenient and fraught with challenges.

Technical fluency. Without exposure to or experience with technology, many women can feel intimidated or resistant to interacting with such an impersonal device. Poor product design can exacerbate the issue with confusing menus to navigate, awkward typing on a 12-key phone keypad, or interfaces designed for nonnative cultures and languages. Women may also not perceive a clear need for ICT and how it is relevant to the challenges they face in their daily lives. One factor may be ignorance about what technology can offer, but another is certainly the lack of applications and services designed to meet women's needs.

Affordability. When prices are high, women are disproportionately impacted as they typically have fewer financial resources than men and less control over spending the resources they do have. Affordability is a particularly big challenge when it comes to the Internet. In developing countries, an entry-level Internet connection costs an average of 112 percent of average monthly income, versus 1.5 percent in developed countries (ITU, 2011, Chart 3.8). Mobile Internet access is generally less expensive, but still unaffordable for much of the population. With such high prices, the Internet remains a luxury good and one that women have difficulty affording.

Coverage. Service coverage and availability of both a basic cellular signal and Internet access remains a challenge, particularly in rural areas. The lowest coverage is in Africa, where just over 50 percent of the rural population is within reach of a mobile cellular network (ITU, 2010).

Limited coverage also disproportionately impacts women, as they frequently have less freedom to travel longer distances and tend to stay closer to their families and farms, while men may seek jobs in the city.

Literacy. When it comes to text messaging, using mobile applications, and going on the Internet, the lower rate of literacy among women is a significant barrier because they are unable to navigate or consume much of the available content.

Numerous programs across the private sector, public sector, and civil society have sought to address these barriers. Under the auspices of the mWomen program, Vodafone Qatar's innovative Al Johara initiative created a network of female sales agents sporting signature red suitcases who sell to other women in the privacy of their homes. The program was designed to empower women while working within Qatari cultural norms that prevent women from communicating with men outside the family. Thus, women are able to learn about and purchase mobile phones in the safety of their homes rather than mobile phone outlets that are typically operated by men. In Iraq, Asiacell, a Qtel Group Company, brought on 1.2 million new female subscribers (a 40 percent increase) in one year by launching targeted services to meet women's needs in the conservative environment. The "Almas" line was designed from the ground up with unique features to match the needs of Iraqi women, such as lower rates for extended calls; free number blocking; and discounted health, cooking, and beauty content. A similar program in Indonesia managed by Indosat, another Qtel Group Company, gained close to two million women subscribers in its first year through a product targeted at stay-at-home moms. They offered a reduced rate for calling friends and family during the day, as well as a family finder service to ensure moms could know their kids were safe.

Recognizing that building technical fluency is a critical precursor to broader adoption of ICT, a number of organizations have invested in technical skills training, particularly for women. With the Telecentre Women: Digital Literacy Campaign, Telecentre.org and the ITU aim to reach one million women through a network of 100,000 grassroots telecenters worldwide. Through this program, Saiyud Phoonsawat of Samutprakarn province in Thailand learned how to use electronic devices, access the Internet, send and receive email, and participate in an online mall where trainees could upload their products for sale—thereby growing her customer base and income (*Telecentre Women*, n.d.).

Similarly, Intel Corporation has developed the Easy Steps program for basic technical literacy education and offers it free to governments and NGOs (nongovernmental organizations). The program teaches adults relevant ICT skills for economic self-sufficiency such as use of email, searching on the Internet, and creating documents.

Affordable Access to Mobile Phones and the Internet

The U.S. Department of State, USAID, World Bank, ITU (International Telecommunications Union, a UN agency), and many technology corporations advocate for government policies and regulations that encourage open markets with healthy competition throughout the value chain, growth-oriented tax policies, and more efficient operations through infrastructure sharing. A more tightly coordinated initiative is under discussion to bring attention and incentives to this complex issue.

The Telecommunications Regulatory Authority of India (TRAI) has been a leader in fostering infrastructure sharing to optimize infrastructure investments, promote competition, accelerate rollouts, and lower prices. Through a combination of subsidies and tax incentives, TRAI has encouraged telecom providers to share passive infrastructure including common-access towers, electric generation sets and connection, site construction, and operation and maintenance. By 2012 (four years from the start of this initiative), the number of towers was expected to go up by 60 percent to well over 350,000 with estimated industry savings of $7–12 billion and ongoing operational expenditure savings of $1 billion a year (Ernst & Young, 2009).

In Africa, Kenya has been a leader in implementing liberalized policies that promote mobile access and affordability. There, the licensing of two additional Mobile Network Operators has increased competition and contributed to a price drop of over 70 percent in four years. Additionally, since a June 2009 government decision to exempt mobile handsets from value-added tax (VAT), handset purchases have increased by more than 200 percent and penetration rates have increased substantially, from 50 to 70 percent (Deloitte & GSMA, 2011).

The high price of Internet access remains one of the most intractable challenges. While much attention is focused on expanding coverage to rural areas, access remains limited to an elite minority even in urban and peri-urban areas where coverage already exists. The high price of Internet access (both fixed line and mobile) has become the leading bottleneck as coverage and capacity improves. Not only does this limit adoption in areas with coverage, but it discourages further investment in expanding coverage.

Rural cellular coverage has been expanding rapidly with significant investments across the telecom industry and development agencies. In 2007, the GSMA announced that mobile operators in sub-Saharan Africa had pledged to invest more than $50 billion over five years to extend coverage to rural areas and roll out mobile broadband services (GSMA, 2012b).

This represents about a fivefold average increase in annual investment since the beginning of the decade and should dramatically increase coverage. At the same time, current technologies can be cost prohibitive to deploy in sparsely populated and poor areas. Organizations such as Inveneo, New America Foundation, and USAID have been experimenting with lower-cost technologies that can overcome challenges in rural environments. In addition, as the Digital Dividend spectrum (freed up in the transition to more efficient digital television transmission) is released for cellular networks, deployment costs can be reduced with fewer base stations needed to cover the same geographic area (GSMA, 2011).

A Tool for Improving Lives

Mobile phones and the Internet can be powerful tools for magnifying the effectiveness of services by speeding up information flow, enhancing productivity, and lowering costs for increasing scope and scale. Simply the ability to call ahead to determine the market price for goods or identify a buyer can increase a woman's productivity and revenues. A phone call can also make the difference between life and death when complications arise in pregnancy. But, beyond a basic voice call, there is the promise of a wealth of services that can touch almost every aspect of life.

One particularly powerful service is Mobile Money, exemplified by Safaricom's successful m-PESA. This mobile phone-based money transfer service has been used by two-thirds of adults in Kenya and has dramatically expanded access to financial services. The impact has been particularly profound for women who have traditionally been underserved or unserved by formal financial services, since 20 percent fewer women have bank accounts in developing countries (Demirguc-Kunt & Klapper, 2012).

Causes for this gap include more difficulty traveling to distant bank branches, lack of property ownership, and indirect asset ownership. Establishing their own financial identity is a source of empowerment for women and opens up self-employment opportunities as well as improved mechanisms for saving.

However, technology is not a panacea. There has been a long trail of ambitious technology pilots that have made compelling demos but have been impractical to deploy at scale. Too often, such projects are overly focused on finding applications for trendy technical capabilities rather than the underlying systemic or human challenges where technology is only one of many necessary tools to deploy. Such services may be developed for mass-market audiences in the developing world where the prerequisite requirements are not sufficiently present. Distributing health, governmental, or agricultural information over SMS (short message service, or text messages) or the Internet requires sufficient literacy, technical aptitude, motivation, and awareness, which often do not exist in the rural areas being targeted. In designing services, particularly those targeted at women, several factors should be considered:

Coverage. For mobile services targeted at rural women, cellular coverage is a key factor for practical use, given the common limitations on women's mobility. Projects should evaluate availability of coverage in targeted areas.

Affordability. If a service relies on mobile or fixed-line data, the affordability of connectivity must be considered, particularly relative to local incomes.

Cultural barriers. Cultural norms in the target community should be assessed to identify potential barriers that may make it awkward or challenging for women to freely use a service.

Literacy. If a service is SMS or Internet based and requires functional literacy, it is important to confirm that literacy rates among the women being targeted are sufficiently high. In many cases, voice-based systems may be more broadly effective. Also, simple icon-based interfaces and local-language video content could improve accessibility. While literacy has been a longtime development priority, it has become ever more critical with the broad range of information available on the Internet. Interestingly, the Internet itself could prove to be a promising tool for teaching literacy, circumventing the limited availability of qualified teachers in low-literacy countries and rural areas.

Motivation. Although ICT holds the promise of accelerating development priorities such as health and education, the reality is that many users are not seeking such solutions. Although 84 percent of poor women desire better healthcare information, only 39 percent express a specific interest in receiving general healthcare information through their mobile phones (GSMA, 2012a). The reality is that Internet access in both the developed and developing world has been driven by social and entertainment applications, as evidenced by the popularity of Facebook, which is perhaps the most common first point of entry. Such services tap into the universal desire for connection and entertainment. Other services are likely to be most successful by working with, rather than against, that reality.

Usability. The steps required to find an application, install it, navigate options, learn syntax, and enter data (especially on a 12-key phone) should be carefully considered relative to the technical sophistication of the targeted women. The reality is that few SMS and Internet services were widely used in developed countries before the advent of smart phones, even though the technology was theoretically available. Women in particular tend to be uncomfortable with the impersonal nature and awkward input of SMS. While 77 percent of women living in poverty have made a mobile phone call, only 37 percent have sent an SMS, regardless of literacy levels (GSMA, 2012a).

Awareness. Unless a service is used daily or pushes content to the user, a key challenge is driving awareness such that a woman will think of the service and know the SMS short code, URL, or application in the moment of need. Spreading and maintaining such awareness, particularly to low-density rural areas, can be extremely costly.

Although less glamorous, basic voice messages or IVR (interactive voice response) can be effective ways to disseminate information to a broad audience, particularly in rural areas where a larger percentage of women tend to be illiterate, have difficulty with navigating SMS interfaces on their phone, or find SMS text messages impersonal. One promising example is the Mobile Alliance for Maternal Action (MAMA), which delivers vital health information to new and expectant low-income mothers through mobile phones. These culturally relevant tips enable women to plan for a safe birth and care for their newborn baby. When both IVR and SMS were offered as options in a Bangladesh pilot, an overwhelming majority of women chose IVR. Aside from transcending literacy challenges, IVR has the additional benefit of enabling more creative, engaging, and richer messages that include music and multiple voices. Systems based on similar technology such as the KACE (Kenya Agricultural Commodity Exchange), Esoko (Ghana), and Handygo (India) provide access to information such as market prices for agricultural produce, weather bulletins, and farming techniques that can help women farmers improve their yields and profits.

Another effective approach has been to equip and train community extension workers with Internet-enabled mobile phones or tablets. These workers are then able to serve as proxies for women, particularly in rural areas, who often may not have sufficient access, literacy, capability, or motivation. The devices can provide them with access to reference information, diagnosis tools, record keeping or data collection capabilities, and the ability to make financial transactions. Training and equipping a limited number of more sophisticated workers with devices becomes much more realistic than trying to serve each individual woman directly. In addition, human interaction can be a critical element when dealing with sensitive topics such as health or finance.

After much experimentation, at least one leader in ICT for development, Grameen AppLab, is now focusing their efforts on solutions that leverage intermediaries.

ICT for Women's Health

Although not directly tied to economic output, the effectiveness of health care services can significantly impact the overall productivity of women and thereby their economic contribution. In particular, women are uniquely affected by health issues related to pregnancy, delivery, and newborn care. A tremendous number of mHealth (mobile health) pilots have been deployed to explore ways that ICT can improve health outcomes. At this relatively early stage, few of these interventions have shown measurable impact at scale, though some avenues seem particularly promising.

As discussed in this chapter, simple notification systems based on IVR and SMS, such as Mobile MAMA, can be relatively simple, yet effective, ways to communicate tips and advice for maternal and newborn health, encouraging women to visit clinics for regular checkups as well as for abnormal conditions. Successes have also been seen in health treatment adherence where reminder messages have reinforced complex drug regimens and scheduled appointments.

Using the extension worker model, the mPowering Frontline Health Workers partnership between USAID and the mHealth Alliance seeks to provide community health workers with mobile access to health information and tools that will expand the coverage of critical maternal and child health interventions. Mobile phones can enable health workers to access life-saving transport, communicate with health centers, assist with diagnosis, and improve data collection.

In a more specialized arena, complex or borderline medical cases outside urban centers can be evaluated by trained medical specialists through remote diagnosis using tools like the award-winning Sana open-source platform. A photograph of the condition can be sent to a central medical facility via a mobile phone or Internet connection, where the remote medical expert can determine whether further medical intervention is required and recommend appropriate treatment. Such systems have been deployed for a range of medical issues from screening for cervical cancer to treating childhood diseases.

While rich applications for smart phones do exist for the developing world, with only 1 percent of the population in Africa possessing such devices, they tend to make better demos than products at this stage. But, with prices of next generation smart phones falling rapidly, increasing fiber capacity coming online, and the hope of reduced prices and increased coverage, the mobile Internet will become an increasingly effective channel to provide information and services in a wide range of domains including education, healthcare, agriculture, governmental services, financial services, and access to markets. For this next generation of solutions to succeed, it is critical that women play a central role both by incorporating the unique needs of women in the application design and by involving women at every phase of the design and implementation of new services.

Economic Opportunities in the Technology Sector

In the United States, although women fill close to half of all jobs in the economy, they hold less than 25 percent of computing jobs. Ominously, the percentage of computer science degrees awarded to women has declined from over 37 percent in 1984 to 18 percent in 2010. And, at more senior levels, the representation of women diminishes to 10 percent of corporate officer and 11 percent of board of director positions at Fortune 500 technology companies, 9 percent of IT management positions, and only 4 percent of senior management positions in technical/R&D departments in Silicon Valley companies (Ashcraft & Blithe, 2010).

This disparity not only undermines opportunities for women, but also exacerbates an economic imbalance as computing-related jobs are growing at twice the rate of other jobs. In the United States, the Department of Labor estimates that there will be more than 1.4 million new computing-related jobs by 2018, and that half of those will go unfilled if current trends continue (Ashcraft & Blithe, 2010). The underrepresentation of women in computing fields is also a significant factor in women's lower income levels, as the World Bank found that the wage gap between men and women is affected more by the lower-paying job sectors women pursue than wage differences between similar jobs (World Bank, 2012).

With ICT arising as a new industry in developing countries, there is an opportunity to recast the cultural perception of the sector in gender-neutral or even women-oriented terms. In many ways, ICT jobs can be ideally suited to women, because these jobs do not require physical strength and can often be structured for flexible hours and locations, thus accommodating other responsibilities women may have in the home and, where culturally problematic, avoiding direct interaction with men. Breaking the male-dominated bastion is important to attract and retain more women in the ICT field, meet the growing talent needs of the sector, and thereby drive overall economic growth.

Unfortunately, girls and women continue to drop out at each stage of the STEM (science, technology, engineering, and math) pipeline in the United States, resulting in an increasing gender gap at higher levels of study and career progression.

Commonly cited reasons include lack of female role models, discomfort in a male-dominated environment, stereotype threat, overt discrimination, family commitments, and overly isolated work (Hill, Corbett, & St. Rose, 2010).

Starting with the transition to secondary education, girls who have shown equal aptitude for STEM subjects begin opting out of STEM studies, often due to social pressures or insufficient encouragement by teachers. This effect is exacerbated at college and graduate levels of study, where the ratio of females further declines. This trend continues in the workplace, where only one-third of women with a computer science bachelor's degree were still employed in a STEM job two years after graduation in 2003 (National Science Foundation, 2003). And more than half (56 percent) of women in technology leave their employers at the mid-level point in their careers (10–20 years) (Hewlett et al., 2008).

Early exposure to technology, curricula oriented around tangible problems rather than abstract concepts, visible role models, and peer support through girls' camps or clubs have all been shown to improve the retention of girls in STEM studies. Professors at Harvey Mudd College found that when they redesigned their introduction to computer science class to use tools that enabled students to write interesting and useful programs quickly, gave students the opportunity to attend a conference for women in computing, and provided hands-on research experiences, they more than doubled the percentage of women choosing to major in computer science (Alvarado & Dodds, 2010). In the workplace, role models and mentorship can also make a tremendous difference by providing inspiration, practical advice, coaching, and connections. They can help women succeed and, even more importantly, help women believe that they can succeed.

Women and Technology in the Middle East and North Africa

Cultural barriers that discourage women from pursuing careers in technology can be particularly pronounced in countries with a Muslim-majority population. To inspire girls in the Middle East and North Africa to pursue higher education and careers in technology, the U.S. Department of State created the TechGirls international exchange program for teenage girls. Through the exchanges, girls are offered hands-on skill building, exposure to innovative companies, and the inspiration of women leaders. In addition, the NeXXt Scholars Initiative attempts to address some of these cultural barriers by encouraging promising girls in Muslim-majority countries to pursue an undergraduate STEM education in women's colleges across the United States and provides mentorship, networking, and skill development workshops through the New York Academy of Sciences.

Further along in their careers, the TechWomen initiative provides emerging women technology leaders in the Middle East and Africa with the access and opportunity needed to advance in careers in technology through a professional mentorship and exchange program at leading U.S. technology companies. These same women may, in turn, serve as mentors for participants in the TechGirls program.

For women in developing countries with fewer educational opportunities, ICT also opens new possibilities for lower-skilled technology-based work that can dramatically increase incomes for marginalized women. Digital "microwork" is one such emerging industry. Companies like Samasource create sustainable livelihoods for women living in poverty with entry-level jobs for tasks such as transcription, cataloguing, and digitization. Workers benefit from dramatically higher and more stable livelihoods, on average doubling their income within six months. Such jobs help women feel empowered, pursue further education, develop marketable skills, and sustainably support their families. Many move on to secretarial or other careers over time, leveraging their newly developed technical skills.

ICT-based enterprises can also provide women with higher and more consistent income streams. Grameen Telecom and Grameen Foundation have been leaders in this arena with the early Village Phone program, which has created 362,000 micro-franchises in Bangladesh and 25,000 in Africa and Asia. More recently, Grameen AppLab has evolved a more sophisticated "business in a box" in Indonesia for selling mobile airtime across multiple carriers as well as other financial transactions such as school fees, prepaid electricity, and motorcycle loans. By January 2012, 9,000 micro-entrepreneurs had been recruited with a total of 27,000 expected by the end of 2012. Such packaged business models give women a clearly defined and low-risk path as first-time entrepreneurs.

Conclusion

Technology is continuing its inexorable march across the globe, transforming the very nature of economies, becoming an essential tool for human and social development, and shifting the skill basis of jobs and professions. In this context, the gender gap in access to mobile phones and the Internet is giving rise to a second digital divide, one where women risk being left further and further behind with lower productivity, less relevant skills, and fewer opportunities. As technology spreads, one must pay close attention to the divergent needs and experiences of women and men to ensure that products, markets, and services are available to the entire population.

Technology is not an end in itself, but rather a powerful tool for improving lives. When applied judiciously, it can reduce costs and accelerate and expand delivery of services that improve women's health, education, business opportunities, and civic engagement. Opportunities also abound directly in the technology sector where job generation is expected to be among the fastest and most lucrative worldwide. The underrepresentation of women in the sector further fuels this digital divide.

Governments, corporations, and civil society all play important roles in bridging this divide. This starts with collecting and analyzing sex-disaggregated data that can yield surprising insights on divergent access, motivation, and usage patterns. Based on this evidence, policies can be better crafted to counteract systemic biases, products can be better designed with real users in mind, and services can be better delivered to circumvent cultural barriers.

As former Secretary Hillary Rodham Clinton noted at the 2011 APEC Women in the Economy Summit in San Francisco, "the increase in employment of women in developed countries during the past decade has added more to global growth than China has." Bridging the gender gap in ICT access, services, and economic opportunities is not only a matter of fairness, but also an economic imperative. It is only by fully and productively engaging the talents and capacity of women that the global economy can truly thrive.

REFERENCES

Alvarado, C., & Dodds, Z. (2010). *Women in CS: An evaluation of three promising practices.* Retrieved from http://www.cs.hmc.edu/~alvarado/papers/fp068-alvarado.pdf

Ashcraft, C., & Blithe, S. (2010). *Women in IT: The facts.* National Center for Women in IT (NCWIT). Retrieved from http://www.ncwit.org/sites/default/files/legacy/pdf/NCWIT_TheFacts_rev2010.pdf

Demirguc-Kunt, A., & Klapper, L. (2012). *Measuring Financial Inclusion: The Global Findex Database* (World Bank Policy Research Paper 6025). World Bank.

Deloitte & GSMA. (2011). *Mobile telephony and taxation in Kenya.* Retrieved from http://www.gsma.com/publicpolicy/wp-content/uploads/2012/03/mobiletelephoneandtaxationinkenya.pdf

du Rausas, M., Manyika, J., Hazan, E., Bughin, J., Chui, M., & Said, R. (2011, May). *Internet matters: The Net's sweeping impact on growth, jobs, and prosperity.* McKinsey Global Institute.

Ernst & Young. (2009). *Wireless Infrastructure Sharing in India* (report).

GSMA Development Fund and Cherie Blair Foundation for Women. (2010). *Women & Mobile: A Global Opportunity.* Retrieved from http://www.mobileactive.org/files/file_uploads/women_and_mobile_a_global_opportunity.pdf

GSMA. (2011). *Digital dividend toolkit.* Retrieved from http://serving.webgen.gsm.org/5926DA9A-2DD6-48E7-BAD4-50D4CD3AF30A/projects/Spectrum/DigitalDividend/DDtoolkit/introduction.html

GSMA. (2012a). *Portraits: A glimpse into the lives of women at the base of the pyramid.* Retrieved from www.mwomen.org/Files/a10df359

GSMA. (2012b). *Taxation and the growth of mobile services in sub-Saharan Africa.* Retrieved from http://www.gsma.com/publicpolicy/wp-content/uploads/2012/03/taxgrowthsubsaharanafrica.pdf

Hewlett, S. A., Luce, C. B., Servon, L. J., Serbin, L., Shiller, P., Sosnovich, E., & Sumber, K. (2008). *The Athena factor: Reversing the brain drain in science, engineering, and technology* (HBR Research Report). Harvard Business. Retrieved from http://rachelappel.com/media/downloads/w_athena_factor.pdf

Hill, C., Corbett, C., & St. Rose, A. (2010). *Why so few? Women in Science, Technology, Engineering, and Mathematics.* Washington, DC: American Association of University Women. Retrieved from http://www.aauw.org/learn/research/upload/whysofew.pdf

International Telecommunication Union (ITU). (2010). *World telecommunication/ICT development report.* Geneva, Switzerland.

International Telecommunication Union (ITU). (2011). *Measuring the information society 2011.* Geneva, Switzerland.

International Telecommunication Union (ITU). (2012). *World telecommunication/ICT indicators database.* Retrieved from http://www.itu.int/ITU-D/ict/publications/world/world.html

National Science Foundation. (2003). *National survey of recent college graduates 2003.* Retrieved from http://www.nsf.gov/statistics/srvygrads/

Telecentre women. (n.d.) (Website). Retrieved at http://women.telecentre.org/?p=1412

World Bank. (2012). *The World Development Report 2012: Gender equality and development.* Retrieved from http://go.worldbank.org/6R2KGVEXP0

Chapter Five

Yemeni Women: The Search for Missing (Lost) Face: A Reading Through the Papers of the Feminist Arab Spring

Arwa Othman, Yemen Studies and Research Center, Yemen

Introduction

Yemen! A country that for centuries has been shattered; divided between south and north, each side with its own sultanates, sheikhdoms, and tribes; and each side ravaged by the other—predominance is the share of the stronger.

In times of crises and rift, the solution has always been either a tribal reconciliation, a truce, or a fragile settlement soon to be shattered by parties engaging—again—in fiercer fighting.

Unfortunately, this has become the image of Yemen, which, in the past, was nicknamed *Alyaman As-s'aeed* (pleasant Yemen). The Yemen of the 20th century and of the third millennium is one of poverty, illiteracy, arms, and drought; Yemen with no infrastructure, no theater or cinema, not even an institute for music. Yemen's natural and human diversity has been reduced to a narrow image broadcasting poverty, a corrupt tribal system, and influential power centers that monopolize the resources of the country.

What are those centers of power that have been controlling the country for decades? The centers of power—the tribe, the sheikhdom, the military, and the religious establishment—belong to the traditional system with its reclusive ideologies. This system dominates all aspects of Yemen. Whenever a glimpse of a "normal" state begins to emerge, or the voice of law is heard, those centers of power unite and attack the rule of law, equal citizenship, and social justice.

The regime of Ali Abdullah Saleh (1978–2012) and the General People's Congress Party (GPC) was established on 24 August 1982 and dominated the Yemeni state and its institutions for more than 33 years. What enabled him to rule for so long was his knowledge of what the centers of influence wanted and his ability to facilitate the achievement of their ambitions. To ensure his lengthy rule, he employed favoritism between tribes and centers of influence, wasting valuable resources—what he called "dancing on the heads of snakes."

During Saleh's rule, in May 1990, the two main regions of Yemen united to form the Republic of Yemen. This move was meant to save both regions, the north and the south. The Socialist Party in the south was experiencing a crisis after the fall of the socialist system in the Soviet Union and the disappearance of Soviet support. In the north, Saleh's GPC was also aging. Hence, both the southern and northern parts of Yemen welcomed unity as an opportunity for increased sustainability. However, this unification was superficial and only served to deepen divisions, and so it did not last.

In the decades following unification, many parties filled the political landscape of Yemeni politics. The Islah Party has emerged as the country's largest and best organized opposition group. Known as a conservative, Islamist party, it is dominated by military and religious figures such as Abdul Majeed al-Zindani, and it plays a major role in the developments of the Arab Spring.

Following the emergence of the so-called Arab Spring and the popular protests in Tunisia and Egypt, the masses in Yemen also took to the streets against Saleh's regime. The war between the regime and the dissenters came to an end during the Gulf Initiative introduced on April 3, 2011, and signed on February 23, 2011. The agreement saved Yemen from impending civil war. It was based on the assumption that what was happening in Yemen was only a conflict, not a revolution that would abolish the corrupt regime ruling Yemen for 33 years and impoverishing land and people. It set into motion the National Dialogue Conference for a comprehensive national dialogue representing all parties. The Yemeni people are counting on this dialogue—scheduled for mid-2013— to get the country out of the current state of crisis.

A Spring That Was Hijacked Before It Even Bloomed

When the crowds went out to the squares on January 15, 2011, all were united in one demand: a decent life in a modern civil state. All were chanting slogans, including "Go away," "The people want to bring the regime down," and "Peace, Peace." The crowd had no single identity: not in what they were about, who they were, what gender they represented, what their political, religious and cultural affiliations were, or what their motivation was. The hero/icon and the commander/leader were absent, there was "no chain," and change was the demand put forth by both men and women of all ages. "In the Tahrir Square, I felt for the first time, that women are equal to men," said Nawal Saadawi, a leading, internationally renowned Egyptian feminist.

This was the bright spot of the Spring Revolution; equality was epitomized in this square, and it represented a new page in the history of mass movements. Unfortunately, barely a few weeks later, the scene had changed, and the Spring had become a camp awash with religious, military, and tribal ideologies, drowning the squares in a flood of rival beliefs: The protectors of the revolution, the people who took to the squares in revolt, and to protect the rebels and the revolution, were actually a dagger in the side of the Spring.

Women Without Faces

In a country where half the population lives below the poverty line and where more than half of all women are illiterate, the lives of women are broken through lack of educational opportunities, a tradition of early marriages, and poor healthcare. Yemen is one of the world's least developed countries, lacking water resources and plagued by drought. Corruption runs throughout the state institutions, and the tribal system dominates on cultural, social, and political issues. In such a climate, in which young girls and women are veiled and restricted from moving about freely, the condition of women remains low and faces numerous obstacles to change and improvements.

Women of 1994—When We Had a Face and an Issue

The "Apostasy and Separation" war led by the Sana'a regime in 1994 in the south, under the slogan "Unity or Death," resulted in a coup overthrowing the peaceful unity achieved in 1990. This was a disaster for humanity in general, and for Yemeni women in particular, both in the north and south. This war bombarded and trampled all the benefits and gains obtained by women in the south before independence in 1967, as they had managed—after the independence—to overturn the family law, which was considered the second most important law in Yemen, after the personal status law. During this war the dominant conservative forces, from fatwa scholars to tribal sheikhs and warlords, led the Parliament, worked together, and betrayed the Constitution by changing its components to suit their ideology and appending the phrase "in accordance with the Islamic Sharia" to every paragraph.

This blatant discrimination was made most clear in the amendment of the "equal citizenship" clause in the Unity Constitution of 1990. Originally, it read: "All citizens are equal in rights and duties without discrimination." It was amended after 1994 to become: "Women are sisters of men, and they have duties and rights as imposed by the Islamic Sharia." Another law preventing marriage of girls under 15 was struck down in 1999, to be replaced by an ambiguous article stating that women can be "married off under any age" in 2010. A draft statute proposed by women's organizations to amend the law to limit marriage to women above the age of 17 was defeated. Parliament has also suspended a draft statute on "secured maternity," which provided important benefits for mothers during pregnancy and childbirth" (Nabila Al-Mufti, paper for the National Commission for Women.)

For decades women had the vote but not a representative, but after the unity in 1990, two (nonsovereign) ministerial portfolios were secured for women: the Minister of Human Rights and the Minister of Social Affairs. In an interim period during 2011 women were given another portfolio, the Secretary of State. In the 2003 elections two women were elected into Parliament, and in the 2006 elections one woman won out of 301 men. The provisions of the Gulf Initiative have confirmed the partnership of women, especially in decision-making positions, to be no less than 30 percent, and in the National Dialogue Committee, during the interim period in 2012, there were six women to 25 men.

The Spring: In Search of the Missing (Lost) Face

On January 15, 2011, Yemen entered the Arab Spring Revolution; the day coincided with Zine El Abidine Ben Ali, former President of Tunisia, fleeing his country. Around that same time, the revolution flourished in Egypt. By February, public squares in Yemen were crammed with women, who, along with men, created the image of the Arab Spring that showed an impressive partnership between men and women—a "no chain" under one clear goal: "To bring down the regime, achieve freedom, effect change, and build a modern civil state."

In Sana'a, Yemen, prayers were even held in one square without the customary barrier between men and women. The erection of the first tent in Al Taghyeer Square in Sana'a in February 2011 had a significant effect on the feminist presence in the square, as it signaled women's full participation in revolutionary activities, allowing them to stay overnight if necessary. Yemeni men, along with their families, were together in the square and shared roles and responsibilities until midnight. This was an unprecedented event in the lives of Yemenis. Some women had even been sleeping in the square since the first day of strikes, and the best evidence for this was the first tent, erected in Al Taghyeer Square, by Farida Al-Yarimi, the first woman to join the sit-in protests in the square. She became the "Mother of the Revolt," as her tent became home to nearly 30 women, and Farida never left the tent for four months. (Following her example, the number of other women's tents started to increase.)

In the revolution square, roles were more or less similar to what happened in other countries that were a part of the Arab Spring, such as cooking food, fundraising, providing medical services, chanting, marching, cleaning of the squares, inspecting, and protecting of women in the marches via the formation of a fence of bodies. There was also high-level work, such as different kinds of photography, the leadership of the demonstrations, and media management, to introduce the Yemeni revolution into the international forum.

The invisible women led and participated in parades with men and were subject to many severe human rights violations. Many were beaten until bloody and accused of treachery and *takfir* (apostasy); some were even martyred in Taiz city, and some women have lost their only providers and their children and husbands. They continued their struggle despite all that. Even when power was shared by the regime and the revolution represented by the Islah Party, systematic violations escalated against the rebels, especially women, so that when women were diversely and uniquely participating in the square, the stronger and more ferocious the attacks on them became.

The first documented violation against women by the regime militants was the arrest of writer and activist Tawakul Karman on February 23, 2011 (as documented in a media report issued by Sana'a University on the same date). Tawakul went on to become the international face of the revolution and to receive the Nobel Peace Prize for 2011, along with two other women's rights activists. The second documented example, also in February 2011, was the physical assault of writer and activist Samya Aghbari and her sister Fatima Aghbari by military forces of the regime (according to an interview with Samya.)

Spring and Its Contradictions: Faces of Ropes and Barriers

In the first weeks of the Spring, the revolution extended from Hurriya and the Taghyeer squares to almost all (i.e., 17) districts of Yemen, and all squares were packed with hundreds of women from different backgrounds. They were subject to visible and invisible harassments and rights violations, but in the beginning such harassment seemed to be isolated cases and not very significant, even if it did sometimes come from the very podium of the revolution (the Islah Party). An example of this is the reference in a speech to "some women who are clothed yet naked," and when the speaker faced opposition from women, another speaker said, "Why are you opposing this; God will not help us when you are like this!" Incidentally, most of the women were covered with the traditional Yemeni veil (*sharshaf*), and only a few were unveiled.

The "Revolutionary" discourse has been, since its first days, an intolerant discourse, in line with the fundamentalist stream that continues even today. From the first day, certain titles and categories of religious identity were used to limit the significance of female participation. For example, women were referred to as the Sisters, the freed, the nobles, the flasks, and the servants of God; the discourse focused on the adoption of the Islamic Caliphate, the remembrance of the Jihadi quest and conquests, the use of systematic miracle-oriented superstitions saturated with the spirit of intolerance, and the self-congratulatory chauvinism of being a part of the "best nation" on the part of advocates well known for their fanatic religious views. What was disregarded was the fact that concepts of citizenship, social justice, equality, civil state, and so on, had vanished. Perhaps the most famous speech representing this intolerant discourse was the one made by one of the Islah leaders and the chairman of the Iman University, Abdul Majeed al-Zindani, on March 1, 2011.

The intolerant and extremist "revolutionary" discourse was violent and aggressive to all who opposed it, and the women of the square were its first victims. Farida Al-Yarimi said, "From the moment I set my tent and decided to stay overnight there, the harassment began, justified under the pretext of caring about us and fearing the regime's military. In the second week, when riots started, and when women began to fill the tent, and insist on staying over with their children, the violence and violations also intensified."

After the first three days of revolution, barriers separating men and women were constructed, beginning with ropes and then bodies— "barriers of Women and Men"—then the segregation reached a peak in March, after the Dignity massacre (March 18, 2011), when "the protectors of the revolution" started to dominate the squares. They were from the dissident army led by Ali Mohsen, the traditional tribes' and sheikhs' forces; religious fundamentalists such as the terrorist advocate Abdul Majeed al-Zindani; other advocates such as Mohammed al-Hazmi, the hero of the early marriage's draft and its legislator in the Parliament; Abdul Wahab al-Daylami, the issuer of the fatwa that urged the killing of southerners in the 1994 war, and many others.

The Rope Tightens

The size of the rope of separation grew and grew as the presence of the "protectors of the revolution" increased in the squares, and the barrier between men and women became more oppressive: guarding and fencing the prayer area; fencing women's gathering areas; tightening access to these areas; monitoring women's movement; searching their tents, buffets, and the field hospitals; and so forth. It started as a thick cloth barrier; then the barrier became a wooden one, then an iron and concrete one, and ended up looking like a cage that is no different from an animal barn, complete with all sorts of prevention and intimidation tools to prevent any man from approaching women.

An issue even more dangerous than these various kinds of preventions and fences is the segregation becoming normal and familiar, as it became normal to see militias from the Islah Party and the Iman University, and representatives of the First Armored Division, wandering about Sana'a with their weapons and batons, preventing integration, ordering people to pray, beating and imprisoning the disobedient, and even accusing people of treason and blasphemy.

As the wall of segregation grew and strengthened, violations against both men and women increased, with women bearing the brunt of it. Many men were arrested on charges of mixing with women and of harassment. The militia invaded the tents on the pretext that male–female mixing was taking place within.

The Invasion of the Tent

The attack on Farida Al-Yarimi's tent has been repeated more than once since the beginning of the revolution in February, because she did not comply with orders. She related, "A woman entered the tent, and closed it from the inside, then opened it from the back adjacent to the wall of the university garden to allow the militia to enter and occupy the tent." Farida had defended her tent; they were coming in with the same reason every time, that the tent was offering places for young men and women to be together in obscene positions, that Farida was an agent of National Security, and that she was somehow compromised. Since the invasion of Farida's tent, the square had seen a number of other invasions (some of which this writer was witness to).

The Separation Discourse: Bombing and "the Invasion of the Bridge"

When the president of the former regime, Ali Abdullah Saleh, gave a speech on April 14, 2011, he said this about the mixing between men and women in Taghyeer Square, "we ask them to prevent the mixing of men and women, which is not allowed by Sharia, in the University Street."

In opposition to his provocative speech, huge demonstrations filled all the Yemeni squares, with people carrying signs saying "Oh Ali the Liar, We Don't Have Mixing," and "Ours is a Revolutionary Struggle, Women with Men," and "Ali Say Something Good or be Silent." In this very demonstration against Saleh's speech, on April 16, 2011, the traditional and *Salafi* discourse in the squares actually weren't much different, except that it was even more backward and barbaric than Saleh's speech. This discourse manifested itself in the famous incident of the "Invasion of the Bridge," where female activists were beaten with rifle butts, shot at, defamed, and accused of treason and blasphemy by the Islah militia (who are a part of the square rebels). These violations became so oppressive that they eventually prevented women from protesting or submitting incident reports; the pretext was that the revolutionary lines must be maintained so that the enemy (Saleh) would not score talking points.

Such incidents, as usual, were not taken seriously and were considered accidental acts and isolated incidents. Having the seriousness of these violations ignored hurt these women's hearts badly and undermined the credibility of the revolution. This pain was reflected in the determination and defiance of the female activists, who stated, "the revolution that beats and accuses us of treason is not a revolution, we want the revolution down." Then the female activists started writing and disseminating statements to different media outlets.

The Large Invasion: "Bushra"

Bushra al-Maqtari, a name that was linked to the revolution since day one, was accused of blasphemy, and a fatwa calling for her death was issued, because of an article she wrote after the "March of Life" on December 20, 2011, about her walking 300 km on foot for five days. Even before that, she, along with her colleagues and other young men, were subject to abuse and accusations from the podium. "Three hundred Islah Party members surrounded us, and attacked us … we wouldn't have been able to survive without the intervention of some people. Then the process of repression and defamation from the podium against me started to increase." The campaign intensified in pace with new ideas coming from the Progressive Youth tent, she continued, "Every time we organized a symposium, we were surprised by the city mosques starting a *Takfiri* campaign against me, accusing me of blasphemy"(interview with Bushra al-Maqtari).

More than 70 religious scholars accused Bushra of blasphemy, and a fatwa was issued against her on January 29, 2012; as if that were not enough, they demanded her life since they considered her an apostate, and asked for the withdrawal of her Yemeni citizenship. They were threatening her life and putting pressure on her family, prompting her to write an important statement about the events, which appeared in many media outlets, including *Al-Wasat* newspaper (July 8, 2012).

The Fall of the Transitional Period

In February 2012, one year after the revolution began, elections were held and a transition was made. However, the campaigns against women did not stop, and actually they intensified against women in the streets, in workplaces, in communities, and in their daily lives. The violations included sexual harassment, early marriage, displacement and killing of women in tribal wars and in the war against Al Qaeda, and even in the wars between the "peaceful" partners of the square—the Islahis, the Houthis and the Hirakies in the south, the former regime, the dissident wing, and the current regime.

The Islah Party militia committed violations against women who were not members of the party, such as Amal Basha, one of Yemen's most prominent advocates for human rights and the head of the Dialogue Committee. She faced severe criticism by the parliamentarian Mohammed al-Hazmi (the man behind the early marriage draft), who said, "How can Amal Basha represent the women's sector in Yemen, if she doesn't veil her face?" (*AL OLA* newspaper, Issue 476, July 8, 2012), he said this while other leading women activists were present in the Dialogue Committee, including Tawakul Karman.

Majeed al-Zindani, an influential militant Islamist, continues to speak and act out against women's equality. For example, he attacks the Minister of Human Rights and civil activists, as well as women's rights organizations, stating that they are agents of the West, participating in the implementation of a conspiracy to secularize Yemen, and are going against provisions of Islamic Sharia law. He has also attacked a group of preachers whom he called "preachers of secularization"(*The Trap of Civil State and Secularization of Yemen*, at http://www.aljumhor.net/portal/news-11635.htm).

The Bombing Discourse in the Aftermath of the Spring

When Jamal bin Omar, United Nations Special Envoy to Yemen, who assisted in the transition of power—described the different parties in power, he said, "they differ in everything, but they all agree on women." He was not being flippant, as it is the reality; these foes/brothers agree only on the lesser status of women. Hamid al-Ahmar, one of Yemen's most influential politicians in the Islamist Islah Party, attacked the women who went to the squares, saying, "there were bad behaviors that transformed the squares into discotheques, these women wanted to go hand in hand with their boyfriends and lovers to the demonstrations, that's against our religion" (interview in the *New York Times*, May 23, 2012). On this, he is no different from the president of the former regime, in that a part of his discourse was directed against women's rights but in the name of law and religion.

The Absent, No

With all this going on, feminist movements and civil organizations were playing a passive role on the sidelines. Bushra al-Maqtari, a leading women's rights activist from the southern city of Taiz, on whom there was a fatwa placed, expressed her frustration at the lack of support from civil society: "Unfortunately, despite the large number of women's movements, civil movements and women's rights organizations, none of them issued a statement condemning what was done to me, or said anything in solidarity with me, nor did my party, the Socialist Party, do anything of that kind. Unfortunately, I felt that everyone abandoned me," she continues, "while others, and I mean those enjoying high positions in the organizations, were using my case before the Europeans and foreign journalists to their own ends, but they never did anything to support me, and I couldn't believe this contradiction" (interview with Bushra al-Maqtari).

Women of the Spring in the Countries of Spring

The conditions of women in Yemen only differ from the condition of women in other Arab Spring countries to a degree, as women suffered greatly across the Arab Spring countries.

We saw the signs of the Spring victorious in some countries, only to see it bringing about its own contradiction; in Libya, just when everyone was relieved that the revolution prevailed, Mustafa Abdul Jalil, Head of the National Transitional Council, stated in his well-known speech, "Any law that contradicts Sharia law will be canceled, and polygamy, in particular, will become legal." This statement was welcomed by the audience with gunfire and shouts of "Allahu Akbar."

The same discourse was repeated in Egypt, for those demanding the cancellation of the women-driven divorce law *Khulu*, under the pretext that it had contributed to the destruction of Egyptian family values. There has been a decline in the awareness of, and support for, feminist thought (Wahid Abdel Meguid, "Women in the Elections Between the Brotherhood and the Salafists, *Al-Hayat* newspaper, December 18, 2011), and the imposition of practices considered human rights violations including virginity tests and the return of female genital mutilation. The new Egyptian government attempted to disband the National Council of Women (NCW), arguing it was a symbol of the former regime due to its association with former First Lady Susan Mubarak. Other issues where backtracking occurred include replacing pictures of female candidates of the Muslim Brotherhood Party with red roses, and justifying that by saying pictures of women are not allowed in Islam.

Who Allowed Her to Go to the Square?

Egypt

When political power reached the hands of the Muslim Brotherhood in Egypt, some started to scream, "Who allowed her to go to the square," "Now you have a president to stop you," and "Stay in your houses," but when Muhammad Morsi was elected to be the president, assaults and violence, including beatings, verbal abuse, and sexual harassment increased, and such violations filled the newspapers and media, as they became a phenomenon that threatened to tear the Egyptian society apart, targeting women in general and nonveiled women in particular. This issue triggered civil organizations to condemn what was being done to women (*Ahali* newspaper, number 1585, July 2012 at http://bokranews.com/?p=22193)

Tunisia

In Tunisia, the Salafi party, known as an extreme form of political Islam, was a driving force behind the movement to veil women and limit their role in decision-making positions, as well as the ouster of the head of the Zaytona religious radio station from her office, claiming that "women are not mentally or scientifically efficient to manage." It is the same stream of thought that pushed for the expulsion of two female schoolteachers teaching Fine Arts, that forced them to recite the "Testimony that there is no God but Allah and that Muhammad is the prophet of God" in public, and to release them only after they received the threat of expulsion (article by Dr. Amal Qarami, "Women And Revolutions And Violence" at http://www.metransparent.com/spip.php?page=article&id_article=16960&var_lang=ar&lang=ar). One of the most serious attempts to decrease women's rights is the move to amend the Constitution to lower the age of marriage and to enable polygamy. Al Bahri Jelassi, head of "Openness and Fulfillment—the National Constituent Assembly amendment to the Constitution," demanded that "every Tunisian man has the right to take a maid besides his wife, and to enjoy the maids he owns." He claims that the "maid" is "the most effective solution to restore balance to the social and moral life of the Tunisian that was damaged by secularism" (http://arabic.upi.com/News/2012/03/07/UPI-93901331124851/). This demand triggered a number of statements from many organizations expressing opposition and disagreement, most notably the statement of the "Tunisian intellectuals," who expressed their fears of making Sharia the main source of authority. "Including Sharia in the Constitution will have a significant impact on the Personal Status Act and mean the loss of equal rights between men and women, for which they have struggled for more than 50 years."

In his statement, Al Bahri Jelassi stated the "reliance on religious rules" and importance of targeting the family law, in an attempt to overturn the legalization of adoption, to stop civil marriages, and to allow marriages by custom, which has in recent years been prohibited by Tunisian law for its prejudicial nature to the rights of women, and because the role it plays in leading to the legalization of polygamy (statement by Tunisian intellectuals in Yemeni *Tajamo* newspaper, number 773–9, July 2012).

There has also been renewed discussion of legalizing the so-called Islamic Awakening, a policy that provides for "farewell intercourse" and allows men to have sex with the dead body of their wives up to six hours after their death.

The Media Coverage of the Arab Spring and the Creation of the "Black Wave" Icon

Local and international media reports were negative in some aspects, and positive in others. They were positive for highlighting the role of women and their participation in the marches, tracking their different activities and participations in events, especially the top-level ones, although the focus remained on the public squares of major cities. The negatives were some media channels, controlled by certain agenda and influenced by propaganda, that only showed women in much reduced roles and in one narrow capacity (the face in black, the masked one, the veiled), depicting what was called the "Black Wave" or the "Black Revolution."

The Icons of the Yemeni Revolution

A main icon of the revolution was the crowd of women, "the Black Wave," which included women from all professions—teachers, housewives, lawyers, legal activists, doctors—all coming out to burn their traditional colored dresses and scarves, to invoke the tribes and their traditions, to protect them from the Ali Abdullah Saleh regime.

The former regime, as well as various political parties, in some cases elevated women members of their parties to create "goddesses of the revolution." These icons gave rise to new slogans and concepts that linked the revolution with a divine right and provided people with a heroic movement to follow.

This approach broadcast to the world an objectified and simplified image of women. One newspaper mentioned that "the events of Yemen are an important mirror to the Spring revolutions in the Arab world" (*Financial Times*, June 4, 2012). Similarly, in an article titled, "The Yemen That Outwitted Us," author Nahla Shahal wrote, "Tawakul Karman emerged and showed women wearing veils and giving statements, displaying an enviable awareness"(*Al-Hayat* newspaper, number 17572, May 15, 2011).

This stereotype of the woman revolutionary leader in Yemen, such as the "iconic" Tawakul Karman (Nobel Laureate 2011), at the head of a Black Wave of veiled women, remains the predominant image of women in Yemen. It also defined the face of political Islam in Yemen, which made the Yemeni traditional veil (*sharshaf*) not only a traditional dress but a religious identity as well, to show the world that the revolution was driven by the Islah Party, the protectors of the revolution, and that the martyrs are the martyrs of Islah—that's what Tawakul Karman stated on her Facebook page, which triggered a wave of condemnation from many other participants of the revolution (http://www.14october.com/News.aspx?newsno=3024415).

Spring of Larger and Deeper Challenges

The challenges faced by Yemeni women are inseparable from the challenges faced by the whole spectrum of the community, as the society at large still has to face its disparate nature, interlaced with reactionary dominant forces (tribal, religious, and military institutions), each controlling and fighting over key national institutions such as legal, political, economic, and education.

Women continue to face tremendous challenges in Yemen and the other Arab Spring countries, including high rates of illiteracy, poverty, underemployment, early marriage, poor health conditions, lack of educational opportunities, and traditions of intolerance and an increase in the number of ungrounded fatwas issued against women. If the feminist movements join forces with the civil forces of intellectuals, liberals, and others, together they could create positive social change.

While the challenges facing women, and society as a whole, intensified with the events of 2011, and whether what happened in Yemen was a revolution or a crisis, hope can be found and built into change if interested parties can agree upon the following goals:

- The empowerment of women, with 30 percent representation in all institutions, life services, power, and decision-making positions, gradually increasing that ratio up to 50 percent.
- Women's participation in the drafting of the Constitution; this is the greatest and the most worrying challenge.
- Reforming the Personal Status Law, which was tampered with in the name of "Sharia," and to restore the "equal citizenship" and the "social justice" laws as stipulated in international conventions agreed on by Yemen.
- Ending the systematic violence inflicted on women in the name of tradition, religion, cultural heritage, customs, and tradition-related taboos.
- Ceasing the categorization of women based on identity, especially religious identity, with distinctive clothing or other different activities.
- Updating the feminist discourse, allowing for fresh blood to be infused into the management of women's organizations, and the uniting of the feminist movements under one alliance to work for women's issues, and to network with women's alliances around the world, so as to benefit from the experience of women's movements around the world as well.
- Restoring our natural faces by closing the doors of fatwas, so that we can see ourselves basking in sunlight.

This chapter was translated from Arabic by Scribe Consulting, Inc.

Chapter Six

The Intersection of Market-Based Approaches and Gender: Turning Ideas into Action

Penny Abeywardena, Clinton Global Initiative

Inside the Clinton Global Initiative

If the world is to mine the untapped potential of all of its citizens and bring greater social and economic progress to our societies, then all sectors—government, business, and civil—must work together. Encouraging leaders within each sector to address global challenges in partnership is the fundamental purpose of the Clinton Global Initiative (CGI).

There are few people who have attended as many conferences or mingled with as many global thought leaders as President Bill Clinton. Therefore, it is unsurprising that he has focused his postpresidency years on convening these leaders through a forum that uniquely requires everyone to do something. Established in 2005, CGI is a global forum for action as well as a marketplace of ideas. Unique from other forums, CGI requires all members to make a "Commitment to Action." From multinational companies to pioneering social enterprises and nongovernmental organizations (NGOs), all members make commitments to address global challenges ranging from education and economic empowerment to global health. Commitments are required to be new, specific, and measurable, and to represent a variety of interventions ranging from traditional philanthropy to restructuring of core business processes and strategies. To date, CGI members have made more than 2,100 commitments, improving the lives of nearly 400 million people in more than 180 countries. When fully funded and implemented, these commitments will be valued at $69.2 billion.[1]

Many doubted the sustainability of a model holding members accountable for turning their ideas into action. Time has, however, proven that members who participate in CGI not only respect a model predicated on taking action but also find value in it. Through the success of the original CGI Annual Meeting (which coincides with the UN General Assembly in New York City), CGI has evolved into a year-round platform with additional brand extensions, including CGI University focused on engaging youth, CGI America which is addressing solutions for domestic economic recovery and our newest platform, CGI International, launched in December 2012.

Girls and Women at CGI

CGI's portfolio of commitments is a veritable gold mine of innovative interventions working to effect social change. Thus, CGI offers a unique opportunity to gain insight and promote an agenda to empower girls and women (G&W). Working closely with members as they develop and implement their commitments, we at CGI gain a valuable vantage point from which to observe commitments that bring about the greatest progress in this space, as well as determine how they are successful. Recognizing a powerful opportunity to inform our largely private sector audience on effective strategies—an audience which was increasingly investing billions of dollars in philanthropic and core business initiatives—CGI began providing dedicated programming on G&W's issues in 2009.

As head of the G&W program, I am allowed an exceptional platform to observe a variety of efforts to develop programming aimed at catalyzing commitments that better integrate girls and women. For the last few years CGI has provided substantive, dedicated programming to issues related to G&W empowerment, ranging from girls' education and maternal health to access to finance and development for entrepreneurs. CGI has also evolved our efforts and gone beyond the status quo of addressing women as beneficiaries of development programs. We prioritize programming that highlights strategies and investments to facilitate and enable women around the world to mobilize and empower themselves and their communities. This focus has encouraged CGI members to identify gaps in strategy on specific issues and collectively catalyze new commitments to action. Members are also increasingly integrating G&W into existing commitments, making their efforts all the more effective. The significant growth in commitments designed specifically with this agenda, to enable and empower G&W, has reaffirmed both the need and value moving forward.

Based partly on the success of the G&W community, CGI evolved its approach to focus on year-round engagement through eight tracks in 2012, one of which is Girls and Women. The primary purpose of this track is to ensure G&W programming is integrated through all of the other tracks: Education & Workforce Development, Energy & Ecosystems, Global Health, Market-Based Approaches, Response & Resilience, Technology, and the Built Environment. This strategy encourages members not actively considering or addressing G&W issues to learn, network, and ultimately participate in efforts pertaining to G&W.

Integration—deliberate and well-engineered—is the way to move forward. CGI does not view G&W as a stand-alone, separate issue, but as a central theme to be integrated throughout our community and programming. This integration provides a more advanced and expansive approach to G&W issues. It is an explicit recognition that any sustainable intervention the global community pursues must thoughtfully address how G&W are involved and enabled. Time will tell, but I believe that promoting a nuanced narrative, to a largely private sector membership, illustrating the role of G&W as drivers of their own opportunity through tools like market-based approaches will offer more impact than anything CGI has done thus far on promoting the G&W agenda.

Track Focus: Why Market-Based Approaches?

In a recently published opinion piece coauthored with Ambassador Melanne Verveer, another contributor to this volume, we argue that women will only get "past the tipping point if leaders across various sectors approach girls and women as actors who drive solutions, not just as beneficiaries who receive their results." Increasingly we see CGI members pursuing efforts through market-based approaches to achieve exactly this outcome, and with success.

CGI's recently minted Market-Based Approaches Track (MBA) works to tackle global challenges by focusing on the issues of financial inclusion, small and medium-sized enterprise (SME) growth, and innovation; redefining the future of capitalism; and supporting emerging trends in impact investing. Within CGI's membership there is significant energy and enthusiasm to capitalize on existing expertise, using new collaborations to engage the market and generate positive social impact across a diverse spectrum of constituents. CGI's focus on MBA as a tool for social change dovetailed neatly with a broader movement focused on women's economic opportunity.

In 2010, the Economist Intelligence Unit launched the first of its kind Women's Economic Opportunity Index. This index analyzed dozens of indicators over five critical areas "to prompt improvements in policy and programs that will encourage women's participation in the workplace and thus create more productive economies overall."[2] This index considers criteria ranging from access to finance (e.g., ability to build credit histories) to women's legal and social status (e.g., existence of laws protecting women against violence). Over the last few years this data set has illustrated a slow and steady rise in the status of women in both the developed and developing world, enabling their participation in economic growth. While the index identifies the important role of government to protect and serve a woman's ability to achieve her economic potential, there are other implicit takeaways. It notably reinforces the considerable and growing role of the private sector and civil society to influence women's ability to become their own change agents, a position CGI has, and is currently, driving through our MBA Track.

I am often asked if there is a silver bullet to women's advancement. An analysis of CGI's commitments portfolio shows that answer as no. That said, the portfolio also illustrates that market-based approaches are a powerful and proven tool that shift the power dynamic. Market-based approaches allow women to access their full opportunity as business leaders, employees, consumers, and entrepreneurs. These market-based approaches are slowly and steadily shifting reality for G&W by providing everything from access to capital and markets, to necessary education and leadership development. This chapter will explore exemplary efforts by CGI members in their use of market-based approaches to enable G&W.

Historical Vantage Point: Avon Cosmetics and its "Granddaughters"

A Model Worthy of Replication

The grandmother of market-based approaches to empower women is without question the inimitable Avon Cosmetics. Over 125 years ago Avon launched its unique model of *business in a bag*, a social innovation that created an army of women entrepreneurs. Their business in a bag model had all the components necessary for an entrepreneur's success: ongoing training, provisioning of finance or consignment for initial inventory, as well as assistance to the entrepreneur in developing a reputation within a community. Avon proved—even before women had the right to vote in the United States—that women entrepreneurs were a valuable investment.

Avon's model has resulted in more than six million entrepreneurs in 100 countries. New research on Avon in South Africa commissioned by the Economic and Social Research Council proves that the model remains effective:

> Becoming an Avon Cosmetics Sales Representative is helping some poor South African women escape poverty as well as inspiring many with self-confidence and hope. South Africa's growing band of "Avon Ladies" are

benefiting from economic empowerment, a sustainable income, raised social status and greater personal confidence.[3]

This study also observed that Black women were earning salaries equal to Black men, a significant improvement in women's economic advancement in certain areas of South Africa. Catherine Dolan, a co-researcher on the study from the Saïd Business School at Oxford, concluded that "many have viewed the global marketplace as hostile to women's interests, but the example of Avon in South Africa shows this need not be the case. We must allow the possibility that the marketplace contains mechanisms, such as entrepreneurship, that can be harnessed for feminist purposes."[4]

This industrious model has paved the path for the next generation of social entrepreneurs to think creatively about how to enable women's economic opportunity in the most difficult of circumstances. While there are a number of excellent organizations working to creatively apply the Avon business model, two CGI members, Living Goods and Solar Sister, stand out from the crowd.

Introducing the "Avon of Pro-Poor Products"

Emerging on the scene a few years ago, Living Goods proudly and loudly claimed its Avon influence by self-identifying as the "Avon of pro-poor products." Focused on reaching the poorest of poor, Living Goods operates networks similar to Avon-style entrepreneurs in rural areas to sell products like iodized salt, bed nets, and malaria treatments. They seek micro-entrepreneurs who are "driven to make a living while making a difference in the community they serve. Some agents were former volunteer health workers who are now eager to earn an income as health promoters. Others ran struggling drug shops with little wholesale buying power and, consequently, meager sales. Living Goods gives these women the opportunity to achieve economic independence by offering them significant earnings opportunities, ongoing training and mentorship, and a flexible work schedule that helps them balance the competing demands of family and farm."[5] They've identified a profile of a worker that stays with the organization long-term, key to their model's viability.

In 2008, Living Goods in partnership with BRAC and Poverty Action Lab, made a CGI commitment to action to increase their footprint in Uganda. Both are extraordinary implementation partners for this program: BRAC is an established antipoverty organization with deep networks within rural communities, and Poverty Action Lab (aka J-PAL) is an esteemed research center based at MIT that is known for its impact evaluation expertise. Through this effort, they aimed to both increase their franchise network and measure the impact of their model on reducing child mortality. After four years of self-described experimenting, learning, and evolving, Living Goods reported impressive results. It demonstrated that it "can deliver compelling health impacts, scale delivery of life-changing innovations, help [its] agents meaningfully grow their incomes, and operate profitable field branches."[6] The results shows that their commitment delivered on expanding their franchise network from 185 communities to 650 in Uganda, and decreased child mortality for 100,000 children under 5 by 15 percent.[7]

Notable to this effort is the partnership with BRAC and Poverty Action Lab, both bringing their distinctive expertise to the table. Its success has resulted in an extension of the collaboration. A *New York Times* piece acknowledges the continuing success of the commitment:

> Despite severe economic distress in Uganda, Living Goods posted its strongest quarter ever in Q4 2011. Driven by innovative marketing, compelling pro-poor products, and strong agent performance, several Living Goods branches broke even for the full quarter—covering the full costs of goods, branch overhead, branch staff, field monitoring, and transport of goods.[8]

Living Goods' version of the Avon legacy illustrates the potential for social entrepreneurs to build on models that work, adapting to deliver results for contemporary challenges and realities.

Living Goods' Micro-entrepreneur Highlight: Sarah Embraces SMS to Better Serve Her Community[9]

Earlier this year, we rolled out a new mobile phone based reporting program to deepen our health impacts and drive more sales to our agents. Our agents in Mafubira enthusiastically adopted the new SMS (short message service) reporting system, led by Sarah Balisanyuka. Sarah has won the "SMS Champion of the Month" for three consecutive months. An impressive achievement in its own right, made downright astonishing after learning that just a few months ago Sarah didn't know how to use SMS on her phone.

Our innovative platform enables agents to enter simple SMS codes to report treatments for malaria, diarrhea, and respiratory infection directly from the field. After agents send a treatment SMS, their client receives a free sequence of automated treatment adherence reminders. Simple reminders to complete the course of treatment can dramatically improve health impact. Agents also use SMS to register pregnant women and newborn children in their community. Once enrolled, these clients receive automated stage- and age-appropriate SMS messages to promote a healthy pregnancy and happy baby. These free SMS services improve our health impact, and they help our agents build stronger customer relationships that drive more treatments and sales their way.

"I really think the mobile system strengthens the relationship I have with the community," Sarah exclaimed. "It adds to the friendship, people get a happy surprise when they receive a SMS from Living Goods, which supports my in-person interactions." But more importantly, "it helps improve impact when we treat malaria or provide antenatal care for pregnant women."

Shaminah is eight months pregnant and just bought a Maama Kit from Sarah. "I think the texts are impressive; no one else does that. I like the info I received about pregnancy and feeding and how to best care for my newborn."

Solar Sister: Avon Model Meets Clean Energy

A few years ago, CGI conducted an analysis of its commitments portfolio to assess how its members were working to empower G&W. We wanted to identify gap areas in strategy to inform our programming and discovered a significant gap in our environment and energy portfolios. Acting on this, over the last few years we have steadily increased our programming and brokered new partnerships with thought leaders in this arena. Through this we found Solar Sister, a young organization with a huge dream. Again using the Avon model as inspiration, Solar Sister aims to create a grassroots clean energy revolution in rural Africa fueled by women entrepreneurs. Through their CGI commitment, Solar Sister has reaffirmed that market-based, women-led distribution models provide the most effective mechanism for training and delivery of their product.

According to UN Habitat, "as much as 1.6 billion people do not have access to electricity, a situation which entrenches poverty, constrains the delivery of social services, [and] limits opportunities for women and girls."[10] Solar Sister recognized the potential of activating women in hard to reach communities because it is these women who "are the managers of household energy use and are the primary customers making usage choices. In order to achieve widespread use of clean energy technologies in addressing energy poverty, women need access to products and knowledge to make informed purchase decisions."[11]

Working with rural African women, Solar Sister is creating a marketplace to enable women as leaders in sustainable solar energy. Consistent with our most successful commitments to action, their efforts rely on public-private partnerships, including the not-for-profit Green Belt Movement founded by Nobel Laureate Wangari Maathai, ExxonMobil, and USAID. Their collaboration aims to expand their Uganda based program to three new countries: Kenya, Tanzania, and Nigeria. Through intensive recruitment, training, and Avon-style entrepreneurial support, Solar Sister seeks to add 3,000 entrepreneurs to their network. Women who would otherwise not be part of the "energy supply chain" will soon be knowledgeable participants providing solar lighting, mobile phone charging, and clean cook stove technologies to an estimated

2.7 million Africans. Solar Sister anticipates that "in addition to greatly expanded access, [their CGI commitment] will bring cumulative household economic benefits of $48.6 million by replacing 198 million liters of kerosene use and mitigating 610,000 tons of carbon dioxide emissions."[12]

Solar Sister, Living Goods, and dozens of others are enabling women around the world by offering economic mobility. A critical component to their accomplishments lies in the model Avon proved successful over 125 years ago. Though it's no silver bullet, utilizing women in market-based approaches is one more tool, or vehicle, we ought to use to assist in raising the aforementioned Women's Economic Opportunity Index, and women's opportunity in general.

Connecting Women to the Global Supply Chain

How Does Everyone Have Access to a Coke?

Most everyone is obsessed with TED Talks. One of my favorites is by Melinda Gates, called "*What Nonprofits Can Learn from Coca-Cola.*" Having traveled all over the world, she made an observation many of us who have the privilege to travel make: Coke is absolutely everywhere. Unlike many of us, however, she connected that observation to the power of public-private partnerships:

> We're trying to deliver condoms to people... or vaccinations. Coke's success kind of stops and makes you wonder: how is it that they can get Coke to these far-flung places? If they can do that, why can't governments and NGOs do the same thing?... It's staggering, if you think about Coca-Cola. They sell 1.5 billion servings every single day. That's like every man, woman, and child on the planet having a serving of Coke every week. So why does this matter? Well, if we're going to speed up the progress and go even faster on the set of Millennium Development Goals... we need to learn from the innovators, and those innovators come from every single sector. I feel that, if we can understand what makes something like Coca-Cola ubiquitous, we can apply those lessons then for the public good.[13]

A few enterprising nonprofits were already working to capitalize on The Coca-Cola Company's micro-distribution expertise. In 2009, the Global Fund to Fight AIDS, Tuberculosis and Malaria initiated a partnership with Coke to deliver vital drugs to the hardest to reach parts of Africa. This commitment to action—to create a scalable and sustainable model that could be replicated by other countries facing similar challenges relating to medicinal supply chains—was announced at the 2010 CGI Annual Meeting.[14] Two years later, the results, which went beyond their initial scope, were reported on stage at the Annual Meeting by Muhtar Kent, CEO of

The Coca-Cola Company. While challenges are naturally abundant, the progress has proved worth the effort: drug delivery times have been cut from 30 days to five, and patients seeking vaccinations find the right one in 80 percent of cases, up from 50 percent two years ago.[15]

A company seeking to improve the effectiveness of their supply chains will inevitably be led to the women in the communities in which they work. The same year Coke entered the Global Fund partnership, it also began the first phase of an ambitious investment to empower five million women in new and existing small businesses throughout the Coca-Cola system (company and bottlers) worldwide by the year 2020. Aptly called "Five by Twenty," this CGI commitment was aimed to "improve the lives of women by involving them in local management and operations; [which] will drive innovations within [the Coke] system, fuel [the Coke] business success, and demonstrate [the Coke] belief in the value of investments in women."[16] This effort, along with other high-profile investments by Goldman Sachs, ExxonMobil, and Walmart, to name a few, began the growing trend of how the private sector uses market-based approaches to empower women along their value chain.

Power of Collaboration: A CGI Commitment to Action Case Study

Research from the World Bank[17] and others prove that the true drivers of the economy are also those least tapped by the market: women—as business leaders, employees, consumers, and entrepreneurs. From a global perspective, Global Entrepreneurship Monitor (GEM) research representing 84 percent of world gross domestic product (GDP) shows that by 2010, approximately 104 million women had started and managed new businesses, adding to the approximately 83 million women leading businesses launched at least three years earlier. Together, these 187 million women demonstrate the enormous contribution women entrepreneurs make to economic growth worldwide. Despite these benefits, women's full economic potential has not yet been realized. Women face barriers when trying to start new businesses or grow existing ones. They experience less access to credit, training, technology, markets, role models, and protection under the law. They also face obstacles—legal, institutional, cultural—that add to the complexity of achieving success, as well as centuries of tradition that define the role of women in the community and the family.[18] Given that CGI members are focused on the largest economic crisis in years, they came to CGI for actionable opportunities to address these barriers collectively.

Driven by the momentum of the crisis and increased member interest, CGI partnered with Vital Voices and WEConnect International in developing new programming. WEConnect International is a recently launched, corporate-led nonprofit that helps to empower women business owners to succeed in global markets. The priority in this effort was to spotlight the role of public-private partnerships in enhancing women's empowerment along corporate value chains. As a result of the first convening, "Strengthening the Supply Chain: A Focus on Women," held in February 2012, multinational corporations, NGOs, and multilateral institutions came together to develop a case study commitment in partnership with CGI. The stakeholders worked with CGI to identify the broad parameters of a new commitment that would be incubated through two years of CGI programming. The commitment-in-development was focused on market-based approaches to enterprise development for the express purpose of increasing the number of women vendors in global value chains. This winter gathering became the first of a series of convenings throughout 2012 dedicated to "Women-Owned Businesses in the Global Economy."

Opportunities for Action

This programming, which will continue through September 2013, seeks to curate conversations that provide learning for neophytes, while also delving into the nuances of existing efforts to explore what works and what does not. The "what does not" part is critical for CGI members in that a number of initiatives tend to start too ambitiously in scale and impact, and are thus unsustainable. We want to encourage members to share their obstacles and lessons learned on the ground, and identify new partners to assist them in completing their project. At the 2012 Annual Meeting, CGI hosted a Commitment Workshop Session on "Integrating Women Into the Global Supply Chain." This Workshop encouraged members to share their experiences designing inclusive supply chains aiming to improve livelihoods and create new business opportunities through the strategic engagement of G&W. In this session a senior executive from Walmart, a partner to the commitment case study, spoke candidly of the challenges they encountered when sourcing from small women-owned businesses. Rather than let these challenges perpetuate as a barrier for other businesses, Walmart chose to share their findings and their process for addressing each challenge with the larger CGI audience.

Through the examples I've detailed thus far, an important and consistent takeaway is the absolute necessity of strong public–private partnerships at every step. The CGI "commitment-in-development" prioritizes such partnerships. Many of the commitment partners have embarked on exciting new efforts, including the following:

> **Building networks to organize women entrepreneurs**: Vital Voices, ExxonMobil, and other partners will organize women SME entrepreneurs through the Vital Voices Businesswomen's Network (BWN), and *will expand the BWN into eight new countries within Latin America, Middle East and North Africa, sub-Saharan Africa, and Asia by the end of 2017.* The goal is to attract and organize thousands of women entrepreneurs at SME level, collecting critical demographic and firm-level information about women

entrepreneurs, and creating an efficient channel to communicate with women-led SMEs who are best positioned to integrate into corporate supply chains. WEConnect International will train and certify the growth-oriented women's business enterprises and introduce them to corporate buyers via their eNetwork platform.

Training for supplier-readiness: With the support of Walmart, ExxonMobil, Goldman Sachs, and the Inter-American Development Bank (IDB), organizations with best-in-class expertise in areas critical to becoming a corporate supplier will provide growth-focused training to women entrepreneurs. For example, WEConnect International will provide training on access to corporate markets and women's business enterprise certification. Verité will lead trainings on incorporating fair labor practices into production processes. The World Environment Center will introduce sustainability best practices within factory environments. TechnoServe will provide sector-specific trainings for agricultural producers. These and other trainings will be integrated into an intensive program that allows women business leaders to understand how to better prepare their businesses for export-oriented corporate contracts. These partners intend to *provide supplier-readiness training to at least 5,000 high-potential women-led SMEs between 2013 and 2017.*

Technical assistance: As part of the McLarty Global Fellows Program, Vital Voices will engage with three schools of the University of Arkansas—the Clinton School of Public Service, the Sam M. Walton College of Business, and the J. William Fulbright College of Arts and Sciences—to provide technical assistance and business advisory services to women-led SME businesses based in Africa and Latin America. Standard Chartered, PricewaterhouseCoopers, Ernst & Young, FedEx, Deloitte Consulting, IBM, and other partners will also provide high-potential women entrepreneurs identified by Vital Voices and CDC Development Solutions with free or low-cost technical assistance delivered through projects that can last between one week and two months. The goal of these programs is to provide individualized assistance at the enterprise level to address critical areas of need that inhibit business growth. Partners intend to *provide at least 60,000 hours of technical assistance between 2013 and 2017, targeting at least 1,000 women-led SME businesses.*

These examples are a few of the many exciting partnerships either underway or in the process of development. CGI's aim in the coming months and years is to support the CGI community as they exponentially increase their investments in supporting women-owned businesses. A sustainable economic recovery hangs on the simple reality that women must be empowered and enabled along the corporate value chain.

Looking Forward

For too long, strategies around women and economic empowerment have ignored the power of market-based solutions. While this approach may not be the silver bullet for G&W empowerment, it certainly is proving to be one of the more effective tools in the toolbox. Market-based approaches is at the heart of unleashing women as entrepreneurs, business leaders, employees, and consumers. The exemplary efforts outlined in this chapter by NGOs, corporations, and multilateral institutions are the beginning of a much larger movement to integrate G&W throughout all aspects of society. Take, for example, the oft underappreciated purchasing power wielded by women around the world:

> In 2012 Unilever made a momentous pledge to make more than half its senior management team female by 2015. Why make such a huge shift to its management structure? Unilever recognized the big business opportunity: "Globally, women control nearly $12 trillion of the overall $18.4 trillion in consumer spending. According to the Boston Consulting Group (2010), this sum of money is more than the GDP of Brazil, Russia, India, and China which was $11.23 trillion in 2011."[19]

The simple recognition by a major corporation of women's global purchasing power will have immense impact on the way it does business—internally and externally. Imagine the impact when these same women are enabled to run their own business or participate effectively in the global economy. Through the MBA track, CGI will continue to offer new opportunities to think and act creatively on this intersection of gender and market-based approaches. While we are committed to existing public–private partnerships that enable women along the corporate value chain and promote innovative entrepreneurs like Solar Sister, we will continue to broker connections, catalyze action, and engage new constituencies in emerging arenas like impact investing and shared value.

NOTES

[1] Clinton Global Initiative website: http://www.clintonglobalinitiative.org/

[2] Abruzzese, L. (2010, September 26). *Empowering women economically: 2010 Women's Economic Opportunity Index.* Retrieved from Vox website: http://www.voxeu.org/article/2010-women-s-economic-opportunity-index

[3] *Avon helps lift African women out of poverty.* (2012, July 2). Economic and Social Research Retrieved from Council website: http://www.esrc.ac.uk/news-and-events/press-releases/21549/avon-helps-lift-african-women-out-of-poverty.aspx

[4] Abruzzese (2012).

[5] *Micro-entrepreneurs making a living and a difference.* Retrieved from Living Goods website: http://livinggoods.org/what-we-do/micro-franchise-business-model/micro-entrepreneurs1/

[6] 2012 CGI PR by LG

[7] 2012 CGI PR by LG

[8] Rosenberg, T. (2012, October 10). *The 'Avon Ladies' of Africa.* Retrieved from Opinionator blog: http://opinionator.blogs.nytimes.com/2012/10/10/the-avon-ladies-of-africa/

[9] *Sarah embraces SMS to better serve her community.* (2012, August 24). Living Goods website: http://livinggoods.org/2012/08/

[01] *Urban Energy.* (n.d.). Retrieved from UN Habitat website: http://www.unhabitat.org/content.asp?cid=2884&catid=356&typeid=24&subMenuld=0

[11] Solar Sister website/Commitment to Action (CTA) form

[12] SS CTA form (link to CGI web page)

[13] *Melinda French Gates: What nonprofits can learn from Coca-Cola.* TED Talks video: http://www.ted.com/talks/melinda_french_gates_what_nonprofits_can_learn_from_coca_cola.html

[14] *Medical Supply Chain Transformation Project.* (2010). Retrieved from CGI website: http://www.clintonglobalinitiative.org/commitments/commitments_search.asp?id=694314

[15] Gross, D. (2012, September 25). *Coke applies supply-chain expertise to deliver AIDS drugs in Africa.* Retrieved from Daily Beast website: http://www.thedailybeast.com/articles/2012/09/25/coke-applies-supply-chain-expertise-to-deliver-aids-drugs-in-africa.html

[16] *Five By Twenty (5X20).* (2010). Retrieved from CGI website: http://www.clintonglobalinitiative.org/commitments/commitments_search.asp?id=695148

[17] *World development report 2012: Gender equality and development.* World Bank. http://siteresources.worldbank.org/INTWDR2012/Resources/7778105-1299699968583/7786210-1315936222006/Complete-Report.pdf

[18] WEConnect/CGI/Vital Voices Concept Note on Case Study

[19] *More women in Unilever senior roles by 2015.* (n.d.) Unilever website: http://acre-resources.com/news/article/2012/09/more-women-unilever-senior-roles-2015?goback=.gde_82951_member_159304121

Chapter Seven

Women and the Global Social Network: Social Media and Women's Economic Sustainability in the MENA Region

Beth Kanter, Social Media Expert

Women around the world are turning to online social networking platforms to launch their own businesses on a path toward economic independence. They are leveraging natural abilities to succeed on the social networking scene and benefit from the flexibility it affords. Moreover, these powerful tools are free to use and easily learned, making possibilities for women in the Arab world and beyond only a mouse click away.

Women Business Founders Take to Social Media to Power Their Success

In 2007, **Evelyn Zoubi** was a student at one of the top technical universities in the Middle East. Evelyn, like many university students and young professional women, enjoyed dressing for success. However, whether she was shopping online or at the Souk, she encountered a challenge when making a new wardrobe purchase. "Would those shoes go with her existing dresses and other accessories?" Since Evelyn was also a techie, she created a software application that allowed her to digitize her wardrobe and potential purchases and then see if they matched.

During her college years, she needed to come up with a project for a course. She shared the software application with one of her professors who thought it would be a perfect project. She started to do more market research and found that her software application had some commercial potential. "At the time, people in my country (Jordan) did not take me seriously. They labeled me as being unrealistic and they laughed at me. They thought of me as some young girl who would create Barbie stuff. After two years, I decided that I would do eCloset (http://www.ecloset.me/)."

She applied for a fellowship as part of the U.S. Department of State's TechWomen program in Silicon Valley and was able to pitch her idea to start up investors.[1] Her goal is to provide digitized closets for women around the world. And while she considers social media important to promote the business, right now she uses it to build her professional network. Says Evelyn, "I use social media channels to help with research for my company and to better understand what women want. I also use it to keep my investors and potential prospects updated."

Noha Mahmoud is a young woman in her twenties and the cofounder of a technology startup in Cairo, Egypt, called Fekra. The company develops web solutions to foster open innovation and industry-academia collaboration across the MENA (Middle East and North Africa) region. As the company's "Chief Networking Officer," responsible for connecting and engaging with current and potential business partners, Noha is fluent at using Facebook, LinkedIn, Twitter, and others to help her company reach its business goals.

She is constantly networking, combining both traditional face-to-face techniques like attending business networking events, meeting people, and exchanging business cards, with online networking techniques. With every connection, she is quick to follow up with an invitation to connect on LinkedIn or find the individual on Twitter and start conversations. As an experienced networker, she isn't just collecting business cards, friends, or followers. She looks at how to build ongoing relationships that support not only her company's business goals, but also her professional career. She is quick to ask herself, "Who do I know in my network that can ..." when faced with a problem to solve for her work.

Using social media to support a women-founded business is not limited to women in their twenties who grew up with the Internet. **Loubna Lahmici** is a 40-year-old serial entrepreneur who lives in Algiers, the capital of Algeria. She attended the University of Science and Technology, where she completed her studies in 1995. Her father encouraged her to realize her dream of starting her own company, and that's what she what did soon after graduation.

Loubna remarks, "In 1995, I started my first company with my sister, who is a systems engineer. We developed custom software programs. Unfortunately, we were ahead of the time. However, we adapted to the demands of the market. This company still exists. It has five full-time employees, and it is now doing well." Since founding her first company, Loubna has started two other technology businesses, one that provides e-learning solutions and online surveys and a company called Dzreduc that offers discounts to Algerian consumers, via its website.

Loubna's business is based on a vision that is both clear and compelling. "I started all of these businesses because I am a new technology enthusiast and because I want my businesses to be in the forefront when e-payment takes over in Algeria. We want to educate Algerian consumers and businesses to bring in more customers and increase their income." And, with the help of social media, her business is not only successful in reaching that vision, but provides a sustainable income for her and her employees.

Loubna uses an integrated strategy for social media with Facebook as the centerpiece. She says, "Facebook in Algeria is the most popular social media platform. It is the right place to be for our business. People are active on Facebook. About 30 percent of Algerian people spend more than an hour a day on Facebook. There are about 4 million people on Facebook. We primarily use fun pages. The way we use it is that we post every special offer and discount on the Facebook page. The reason we do this is because we don't wait for the members to come and visit the website. We push the information to them. This way, they can get more details about the offers and download coupons. What is great with Facebook is that it is viral. If people like our offer, they can share it on their page and attract more viewers."

Women entrepreneurs outside of the technology arena are also turning to social media. **Nour Bouakline** started her blog to share her passion for food in 2010. She used the blog to share recipes, tips, and pictures of her creativity with Tunisian cuisine. She moved to writing in food columns for online and print magazines including *Sanafa* (which means "good cook" in Tunisian Arabic). She also launched her Facebook page and built an online community of her fans. She uses social media to market her skills and regularly receives requests for cooking assignments in her community.

Noha, Nour, Evelyn, and Loubna represent a new breed of women business founders who are not afraid to think big and use social media and networks to achieve success. They are four women among thousands in the MENA region who are embracing Twitter, LinkedIn, and other social platforms to launch and promote businesses every day and network their way to economic independence. The "Most Influential Women in the Arab World on Social Media" lists and "Top Arab Women on Twitter" (www.twitter.com/#!/Shusmo/top-arab-women-on-twitter) reveal a vast diversity of successful women business owners of all types and sizes, from online technology to catering companies.

Women and Principles for Effective Online Social Networking

Women are well-equipped to thrive in this digital age and run successful businesses because they typically possess the skills necessary to develop and execute social media strategies successfully. At their core, the techniques I teach in workshops around the world rely on strong communication, listening, collaboration, and the ability to invest time and resources wisely. Below, I take aspects of that curriculum and write about the characteristics that power those basic techniques.

Women As Communicators

Loubna Lahmici, who has used social media extensively to promote her technology companies points out, "What is important is how you interact with friends and followers. It depends on the skills of the community manager, not necessarily the gender. But, when a woman manages our Facebook page, they are more expressive and open."

Key strategies for successful online networking rely on quality, lively, and consistent communication. One such tactic is getting the community to participate with your brand. This can be through letting fans provide information, or just promoting maximum participation with comments and two-way communication. "Show me your Mumu" effectively uses the Facebook page to engage their clients (www.facebook.com/showmeyourmumu).

Another strategy with communication at its core is providing fans with deals. Giving coupons and other breaks can be a good way to reward fans. Consistent discounting carries the risk of potentially devaluing your brand, but can be avoided by creating a separate account for discounts. Some brands have opened a Twitter account that carries nothing but the latest deals (see @delloutlet), and Sprinkles Cupcakes (www.facebook.com/sprinkles), drove more than 50 additional people in each store location through "whisper codes."

Loubna Lahmici is currently using Facebook for the Dzreduc discount website (www.facebook.com/Dzreduc). She says, "We post useful content on a regular basis, at least once a day. We ask people for their needs and expectations and try to exchange dialogue with them. Your messages shouldn't be entirely focused on your business all of the time. For example, for New Years, Ramadan, and Eid, post greeting messages. Try to be funny, nice, and likeable. In social media you have to establish a business relationship but also a social one. People shouldn't feel like you are only trying to sell them something. They should trust you."

Successful entrepreneurs who use online social networking tools don't just put up a social profile and abandon it. They understand that if they don't keep it fresh, they'll do more harm than good to their brand and customer experience, leaving potential customers wondering what else they might leave neglected.

Blogs are another platform through which women excel at interacting and engaging with fans. There are many different ways to use blogs to support business goals, from sharing product development news as it happens to providing resources and how-to information. Blogs can be platforms for thought leadership or show off business expertise, and they offer fertile ground for sharing stories of customers. They enable visitors to leave comments, providing an interactive forum for dialog, and many are free to set up (via Typepad.com or other websites).

Blogging isn't just about writing content for someone to passively read— the goal is to get readers to discuss the topic by making comments, sharing their insights and anecdotes, and telling their friends. It's all about engaging your audience in a dialog—with you and with other readers. Blog posts that are good conversation starters are not comprehensive, leaving gaps for readers to fill in, and many have a question in the title, or at the end ("What do you think?" works wonders). Posts are generally written in an intimate, informal style, as if you were sitting at a café table having a conversation. It certainly isn't the institutional boilerplate, which is a huge conversation stopper.

Women As Listeners

Entrepreneurs who are successful at embracing online social networking tools have a deep understanding of their current or potential customers. They listen to who is engaging and what they are saying, and respond to customer needs, and build more effective teams of employees, contractors, and partners. In fact, many women entrepreneurs often describe building their business as building a team. People create the basis for an entrepreneur's content and choice of tactics so listening is key to developing strategy.

Sanae Baatti is planning to launch a business that sells monthly subscriptions to online software as a service to manage law firms. Sanae describes the value her business will provide to customers: "Our service guarantees the user mobility since the access is tied to the individual not the computer, low cost of entry and lower total cost of ownership, [and a] simple and secure management system. We combine leading technologies, creativity, and understanding of clients' requirements to produce software that unlike any other in the market is reliable, user friendly, and cost effective." She is planning to use social media as a tool to connect and interact with her customers to better determine what they need and how to improve her software products.

Loubna Lahmici says that staff at her company Dzreduc often ask people what kind of offers and discounts they want, find out what their favorite brands are, and listen to any feedback from customers. Says Loubna, "We then go to the brands and negotiate discounts. When you listen to people, you can adapt your offers and create new services and new products—and that helps you be more successful."

Women As Collaborators

Women have worked well together since the earliest female enterprises, whether dividing grains in the village or working in crafts cooperatives. Women are consensus builders, conciliators, and collaborators, and they typically employ what is called a transformational leadership style—heavily engaged, motivational, and extremely well suited for using social media.

According to Evelyn Zoubi, founder of eCloset, "Men and women think differently." She asserts that women have much more influence over civil society. "Even if we want to have a political change or a change in technology, women are the influencers. We should be united and be together. I never knew I could get support from a community of women, but I did. Women, they understand each other's emotions and dreams, and they influence a lot of people as a result." In fact, a very popular strategy is for companies to work with influencers (usually bloggers and people with a large social presence) to showcase products and services. Usually this requires finding bloggers who write about relevant work. The best way to get a blogger to show interest is by creating an experience for them, for instance, gathering local bloggers to discuss an issue that tangentially relates the product or service being marketed.

Social media platforms offer many opportunities to connect with other professional businesswomen to share stories, trade advice, and support one another. Evelyn Zoubi (eCloset) observes that her experience participating in the TechWomen Program was critical to her success. She says, "Ultimately, in the program, we were inspired by each other and the different fields we came from. The women inspired me in my business. The diversity in technology, it ignited and triggered some thoughts." While formal networking programs and projects that bring together women business owners for training, support, and mentoring offline and continue the networking online are ideal, women can also build their own support network by using tools like Twitter and LinkedIn.

Loubna, also a participant in TechWomen says, "After TechWomen, I learned to set up a vision and think big; it gave me the opportunity to visit Silicon Valley and meet with amazing people and visit Facebook and Google, which was a dream. I think also it allowed me to connect with my counterpart within the MENA region. I returned home with a lot of projects and new insights on how to use different tools."

These stories represent another important aspect of effective online social networking: community building. This is the process of engaging current and potential customers around a product or brand. It takes time, but ultimately generates a lot of word of mouth referrals for a business. *Sanafa* magazine (www.facebook.com/Magazine.Sanafa or www.facebook.com/randotunisie) and *Association Tunisienne des Randonneurs* (www.randotunisie.tn/) are great examples for understanding community engagement through Facebook pages.

Women As Conservative Decision Makers

Women typically are more risk-averse or conservative than men, and the digital age offers a wealth of low-risk opportunities. Ventures like blogging, web-based services, and ecommerce and software development require smaller upstart costs than manufacturing-based, brick-and-mortar type businesses. Cloud-based tools and virtual workforces further lower the cost of entry, making the idea of starting a business more feasible and palatable.

Using social media is an inexpensive and easy way to grow sales; however, it is important to have a strategy behind the choice of tools. As many women entrepreneurs know, starting or running a small business takes time and resources, so it is important to take a selective approach, focusing on adopting different tools or one tool at a time and only the tools that make sense to reach their target audiences. While women business owners won't need to hire a full-time person to do their social media or spend all their time on LinkedIn, they will need to spend time finding or creating content to share, maintaining their networks, and being comfortable with the tools. In addition, customers are becoming accustomed to rapid responses if social media channels are open, so successful women business owners seek out the best tips so they are efficient.

Somaya Momani started working five years ago as a tailor. After a year, she decided to widen her network and establish her own business (http://aumallolo.blogspot.com). As a participant in the E-Mediat program, she learned how to use social media as part of promotion and marketing plans.[2] As a result, she was about to reach many more potential customers, most of them women. She says, "Using the Internet and social media to market my business allowed me to be more efficient in my outreach."

These women understand that social media present an amazing opportunity for women-run businesses, leveling the playing field and bringing growth to those who really deserve it. The successful women understand that it requires a commitment and thus do not attempt to take on something that they cannot sustain.

Online Social Networking and the Mobile Office

Digital and social media tools mean that women can now build a business from home, create unique work schedules, and do so without large start-up costs. Virtual workplaces and digitally mobile lifestyles also give aspiring women entrepreneurs the flexibility to achieve a balance between work and family responsibilities. By its virtual nature, social media has the potential to remove social and religious barriers by making first interactions about the business, and not the stereotypes associated with the person behind the business. It also provides the opportunity for women to not have to seek permission from a father or husband when wanting to start up a business online. It should be noted that though social media provides an exciting platform for women to grow their own business and economic independence, the necessary start-up cost of owning a computer with reliable access to the internet is still limited to those of a certain economic class. While it may not reach all socioeconomic classes, social media still provides immense opportunity for many.

Conclusion

Facebook is the largest online social network in the world. It reached 1 billion users in October 2012. The United States remains on top, with 166 million users, and is followed by Brazil and India. Egypt remains the top Facebook nation in the Middle East region and managed to overtake Venezuela and Chile to clinch the 20th spot in the list, thanks to its 108 percent growth. Users in the Arab world are growing and estimated at over 20 million in 2011 according to the Internet World Stats (www.internetworldstats.com/stats5.htm).

Online networking platforms, like Facebook, are powerful tools that are readily available and accessible to those who know how to use them effectively. In the coming era, as we look toward women to be the major drivers of global economic growth, online social networking tools will be crucial to making this happen and maximizing the impact.

NOTES

[1] An initiative of the U.S. Department of State, Bureau of Educational and Cultural Affairs, TechWomen brings emerging women leaders and entrepreneurs from the Middle East and Africa to the United States for a professional mentorship and cultural exchange program, where they are paired with their counterparts in San Francisco and Silicon Valley.

[2] Mediat is a technology training and capacity building program developed in response to Secretary Clinton's announcement of Civil Society 2.0, an initiative which helps grassroots organizations around the world use digital technology to tell their stories, build membership and support, and connect to their community of peers around the world. The program builds the capacity of local organizations to advocate for their work, sustain their programs, and find creative solutions to shared challenges. E-Mediat is funded by the Middle East Partnership Initiative (MEPI) of the United States Department of State with support from the craigslist Charitable Fund and Microsoft.

RESOURCES

Noha's Twitter profile: https://twitter.com/NohaMahmoud

Noha's LinkedIn profile: http://www.linkedin.com/in/nohamahmoud

Noha's Blog: http://egypttechdays.blogspot.com/

Fekra's web Site and Social Media Profiles: http://www.fekra2.com/

Nour's personal Facebook profile: https://www.facebook.com/nourbouaklinezi

Nour's Facebook Page: https://www.facebook.com/pages/Un-peu-de-tout-beaucoup-de-moi/172771886103523

Nour's Blog: http://un-peu-de-tout-beaucoup-de-moi.over-blog.com/

Facebook page of *Sanafa* magazine: https://www.facebook.com/Magazine.Sanafa

Tendances: http://www.tendancemag.com/

https://twitter.com/NadaAbandah

http://about.me/nadaabandah

https://www.facebook.com/IntrinsicTips

https://twitter.com/ZeinabSamir

http://about.me/zeinab

http://www.supermama.me/

http://profile.typepad.com/omnentrepreneur

https://twitter.com/OmnEntrepreneur

Chapter Eight

Expanding Women's Access to Capital and Financial Services

Mary Ellen Iskenderian, Women's World Banking

The World Economic Forum's *Global Gender Gap Report 2011* reports that on average, international scores for health and education are encouraging with 96 percent of the health gaps and 93 percent of the education gaps already closed. Around the world, economic and political participation continue to show the largest gaps (Hausmann, Tyson and Zahidi, 2011). According to the report, "The correlation among competitiveness, income and development and gender gaps is evident.... While correlation does not prove causality, it is consistent with the theory and mounting evidence that empowering women means a more efficient use of a nation's human talent endowment and that reducing gender inequality enhances productivity and economic growth."

There has been much research done about the potential impact of women's participation in the economy—both as producers and consumers. The World Bank estimates that the Asia-Pacific region was shortchanged by $42–47 billion because women's economic potential was not fully utilized. To put this in context, that would have contributed another 1.5 percent annual growth to the region's economies. Women now represent 40 percent of the global labor force, 43 percent of the world's agricultural labor force, and more than half of the world's university students. Eliminating barriers that discriminate against women working in certain sectors or occupations could increase labor productivity by as much as 25 percent in some countries.

Financial institutions can play an important role in closing the gap in economic equality. Women need access to the means of production, which means loans for small businesses or the ability to save for building a business. For women who have been shut out of the formal economy, the opportunity and the tools and means of production allows them to become economic agents for the first time. It also gives women a safe place to save.

Listening to Women

Beyond the GPD and productivity gains, there are social implications for investing in women. Because of her role as caregiver, when a woman generates her own income—and this holds true no matter what the country—she reinvests her profits in ways that can make long-term change across the generations: in the education of her children, healthcare for her family, and the quality of her family's housing. Given these are the financial priorities of women, we at Women's World Banking (WWB) know that women need more than loans, which we typically associate with microfinance; and they need access to a safe and secure place to save, insurance products, and pensions—the same financial products we all need.

In order to integrate women into the financial sector, we have to understand their lives: the cultures in which they live and work, their role as caregiver, and their financial needs and goals. We must acknowledge that they often live and work within cultural constraints that affect their ability to access financial services or grow their business. For WWB this is why customer research is so vital. Listening to women about their financial lives is at the heart of our research, and they tell us that there are major barriers for poor women that impede their inclusion in the financial sector. Understanding the lives of women and the challenges they face is imperative to closing the financial inclusion gap. WWB's success over the past 30 years has been based on our ability to understand customer needs and develop appropriate, responsive solutions.

Our approach to market research, the foundation of all our projects, involves going beyond simply asking about preferences and money management to exploring underlying factors such as cultural patterns of gender, identity, status, and household relationships that we find to be critical in delivering tailored financial services to women. WWB then uses insights from this research to inform all of its work. This chapter draws upon qualitative market research conducted by WWB between 1999 and 2012 with 18 of its network member microfinance institutions (MFIs) in 17 countries. Five studies were conducted to inform the design of women-focused credit financial products, and seven gender baseline studies were conducted to help understand how gender identities, roles, and responsibilities inform intrahousehold resource allocation. The populations studied include former, current, and potential borrowers of MFIs. Data were also drawn from quantitative research conducted with several WWB network members.

Our research has formed some of the cornerstone findings that drive much of our product development. For example:

- Women's earnings are viewed as "supplemental" to men's, leading to a tendency for women to divert money from their business to household needs, while men can reinvest earnings in their business to help it grow.
- WWB finds that while women have entered the productive sphere, men have not correspondingly assumed more of the household responsibilities.
- Mobility constraints lead to women's involvement in predominantly home based businesses, which are in highly competitive sectors and require limited human and investment capital. Businesses are often extensions of household activities, such as sewing, buying and selling goods, running beauty parlors, and catering. While these activities have low barriers to entry, they also have limited scalability. Additionally, lack of mobility limits the customers with which women can do business (i.e., selling to neighbors on credit rather than receiving cash) and leaves male household members to buy and sell in the marketplace, consequently allowing them to assume greater control over the business and its profits.
- Reaching women in rural markets presents an additional set of challenges. Research by WWB in Uganda (Banthia, Green, Kawas, Lynch and Slamas, 20011) found that women in rural areas tend to be unpaid laborers on family farms, but also engage in their own small-scale income generating activities. However, these activities are viewed as supplemental, and financial institutions often reach out to rural markets only through male dominated agricultural co operatives that leave women farmers ignored and unserved.

Ensuring that women have access to enterprise credit requires that we start with a framework of understanding these findings. We can then tailor the way banks interact with customers, how products are delivered, and the attributes they must encompass to appeal to women.

Expanding Credit for Women

Microcredit, as developed in the 1970s in South Asia, is a model based on group lending, in which the collateral is the group's promise of repayment. As the industry matured, it became clear there was demand for an additional form of lending based on business income or other collateral. In the early 2000s, WWB introduced appraisal based individual lending practices into nine MFIs that had previously practiced group lending. Each MFI wanted to offer a product that would allow its clients to grow and would offer the MFI an opportunity to enhance its organizational capability and competitiveness. However, WWB found that only a small percentage of group lending borrowers had a microbusiness capable of supporting the type of individual loans commonly considered to be best practice. This approach requires that a business generate sufficient profit to pay the majority of household expenses and reinvest in the business, and few women meet these lending criteria. WWB found that a notable glass ceiling existed in the informal economy.

Research has shown that two segments clearly exist among MFI clients. The "income generation" segment is typified by borrowers with income generating activities that are most often home based, with seasonal income and sales based on credit rather than cash. Women entrepreneurs dominate this segment. The second segment is what WWB calls the "microenterprise" segment, where one business generates the majority of income for the household. These businesses are often located outside of the home, sales are based on cash, and revenues tend to be less subject to seasonality. Male entrepreneurs tend to dominate the microenterprise segment.

There are many reasons for this stratification, including those previously mentioned—time constraints, lower education levels and literacy rates, and the perception that women's income-generating activities are secondary or supplemental to men's. Women tend to grow their businesses horizontally by investing in a number of income generating activities, rather than expanding a single business, in order to diversify risk and ensure steady cash flow throughout the year. This diversification allows women to take advantage of seasonal opportunities, but limits the growth of any single business. Understanding these differences provides an opportunity for financial institutions to better serve women with new approaches.

One of the emerging areas in which modifying a generic credit analysis and loan structure could increase access for women is the agricultural sector, where cultural perceptions are keeping women from realizing the potential of their business. Rural women, who make up one of the largest and most underserved segments of the world's poor, face the greatest barriers to entry into the financial system. They face greater mobility constraints than urban women and tend to be less educated. Income-generating activities generally split along gender lines in rural households. Men are the authority figures, main financial providers, and managers of the family farm, while women are the homemakers and caregivers and often serve as a key source of labor for the farm. Rural women tend to engage in supplemental-income-generating activities, such as selling extra food crops, milk, or eggs; cooking; or making handicrafts. These are typically low-paid activities that are viewed as extensions of women's household activities. This can make the economic contribution of women practically invisible. WWB has found that women often do not identify themselves as important contributors to the household income even in situations where they contribute a significant portion of household income. During 2011, WWB conducted research in Paraguay and found that agricultural activities managed by the husband were overestimated by loan officers, while the non-farm income-generating activities managed by the wife were not analyzed correctly and were significantly underestimated.

There are several potential solutions: for example, training loan officers in whole family analysis and adjusting product features to ensure that they work for women. The more difficult challenge is changing the way women's work is valued. One proposal is to encourage the financial institution to initiate a major marketing campaign that helps to make women's work visible. WWB has had success with this approach in several markets. In 2006, WWB partnered with the Microfund for Women (MFW) in Jordan on a similar project that positioned entrepreneurs as ambitious self-sufficient women, described in the accompanying box.

Box 8.1: Empowering Every Ambitious Woman

Women's World Banking gender research in Jordan found that despite women's important financial contributions to the household, Jordanian women and men rarely acknowledged women's roles as "businesswomen" with pride. Women were often derided for their work or made to feel as if their work was unimportant or secondary to a man's work. "[I wish that] people don't make fun of us for what we do, that [they would say that] what we do is actually worth something," said a woman respondent. Seeking to change these perceptions of women and to build its reputation as a top-choice MFI for women, WWB network member Microfund for Women (MFW) in Jordan embarked on a national social advertising campaign with the international advertising agency Saatchi and Saatchi. The campaign used the slogan "Empowering Every Ambitious Woman," which strongly resonated with women. "[I am] proud and happy that the woman is now working and that the woman has progressed from a long time ago," said a woman respondent. The campaign utilized television, billboards, bus wraps, posters, and brochures to communicate this powerful message, and it won Jordan's Media Award for Best Press Campaign in 2006. It also helped to establish MFW as an institution that cares about women and as a market leader.

"When I see the ads, I feel proud I've taken these loans from MFW."

—*Client of MFW*

"You feel that when a woman does something, there is actually something that comes out of her efforts."

—*Client of MFW*

One of the challenges of including women in appraisal-based individual lending is adapting loan requirements to make them accessible to women. Many institutions still require collateral, such as a property title, to which women, particularly rural women, often do not have access; or they require a co guarantor. Less than 1 percent of the world's land is owned by women. If financial institutions want to reach women, they have to understand how to modify collateral requirements and, where possible, help women achieve joint ownership of marital assets.

Microfinance has been effective in some markets because of its ability to go directly to clients. Institutions understand that serving women often means providing services in their communities and homes. Women put a real premium on time, and time spent at a bank branch or at a group meeting is time away from their businesses and household duties. The responsibilities of childcare and maintaining a household already significantly limit the time women have to devote to their businesses. Institutions can better serve women by keeping group meetings shorter or less frequent and by making transactions at the bank branch more efficient.

Beyond Credit

Increasing women's access to capital can help close the productivity gap. There is, however, much more to full financial inclusion. Are we giving the poor the tools to build assets and protect against loss? Any productivity gains could be wiped away in an emergency—food crisis, drought, health emergency, or any of the other economic shocks that can upend a family living on $2 a day. One of the most important products we can offer women is access to a safe place to save. WWB knows from its research that poor women are inherent savers but are forced to save informally in unreliable ways: in a tin can or buying excess stock for their business when they don't have access to savings accounts, because either they can't get to a bank or the bank isn't interested in serving their needs. While their financial lives are complicated—juggling subsistence needs, emergency expenses, and school fees with an unpredictable income—they still manage to save on average 10 to 15 percent of their income.

Savings Mechanisms for Women

When developing a savings product for women, product attributes are even more important if clients are going to move from informal to formal savings mechanisms. Through research conducted in 10 countries, we know that there are very basic attributes critical to women when deciding whether to save with an MFI.

- *Safety:* Women want a savings vehicle safe from theft and coercion by family members, including spouses.
- *Confidentiality:* Women want to decide whether or not to share information about how much and what they are saving with husbands, children, or in-laws.
- *Convenience:* Women need a way to make small, frequent deposits without taking time away from their domestic responsibilities or from running their business. Allowing women to deposit regularly, including weekly, can really help them save. See the accompanying box titled "Alternative Delivery Channels" for more information.

Box 8.2: Alternative Delivery Channels

Mobile phone technology and other alternative delivery channels (ADCs) have the potential to go further in giving women greater control over their financial futures by giving them direct access to financial services. The emergence of the cell phone as a low-cost means to conduct financial transactions represents a significant breakthrough in democratizing access to financial services. Additionally, ADCs can allow MFIs to reach more remote markets that may otherwise be too costly or difficult to serve. Further research is required to fully understand how technology can be used to benefit women's access to financial services. WWB is testing ways that local merchants can use to accept deposits through point-of-sale terminals, as well as using mobile phone banking as a real tool for savings. Going beyond the conventional local branch to bring the bank to women facing mobility constraints can have a major impact.

- No fees or penalties: In many countries where WWB has done research on savings, low-income customers tend to distrust banks because of fees that erode their savings and are poorly understood. Network members, including Banco WWB in Colombia, are working to develop simple and accessible savings products that can be understood by customers who are not accustomed to saving at a bank while building trust in the process. Simplest and most effective of all offerings are no-fee accounts that let women access their money when they need to without penalties. To make this approach sustainable, however, institutions must invest in cost-effective approaches to managing savings.

Financial Education

While it is clear what clients want, the real challenge is in creating a product that is sustainable for MFIs. Offering a savings product requires a fundamental shift in perception by both clients and institutions. Leaders need to align the institution's staff around this new vision and strategy. WWB network members, as leading MFIs, have high recognition among their target customers. When they expand to offering savings, they need to reposition themselves as a safe place to save, in addition to being a loan provider. Savings also requires further investment in financial education.

WWB is committed to embedding financial education in all of its products and has adopted varied approaches to deliver financial education. For example, in collaboration with the Self-Employed Women's Association (SEWA) Bank in Ahmedabad, India, WWB developed and piloted a new process to systematically embed financial education into existing interactions between clients and the bank, for example, via marketing materials or when savings and credit officers visit clients at their homes. This approach allows the delivery of short, frequent financial education messaging on a small scale, on occasions when clients are open to receiving them, rather than trying to fit classroom trainings into their lives. At SEWA there are almost three times as many customers with savings accounts as borrowers, and the bank has set the ambitious target of serving one million savers by 2015. Project Samruddhi is a two-year collaboration between WWB and SEWA Bank to help increase the number of women who have savings accounts and the frequency with which they save, through financial education and marketing. One of SEWA's hallmarks is its *doorstep* banking—run by women from the community, known as *saathis*, who act as credit and savings collection officers. Customer research showed that strong, personalized *saathi*–customer relationships can be very powerful, for both the customer and SEWA. Customers almost unconditionally trust their *saathis*, open the accounts that are recommended to them, and follow instructions to qualify for loans if so desired. A *saathi* may visit up to 50 clients a day, and she also reinforces the concrete, relevant, and actionable financial education messages that customers receive in classes with everyday interactions, often delivered via iPod Touch, yielding the potential to help women set and meet long-term savings goals.

WWB is also testing the effectiveness of social soap operas in other markets to communicate the importance of saving with a financial institution. In the fall of 2011 WWB launched its newest initiative to encourage women of the Dominican Republic to become better money managers, to build savings, and to create a more secure future for themselves and their families. The groundbreaking socially minded soap opera, *Contracorriente*, produced by and in partnership with Puntos de Encuentro, explores the ways in which media can positively influence financial behavior. The series exposes low-income women to intimate and complex topics such as money management and dealing with household financial dynamics, embedded in the traditional story lines of a soap opera. During its first run, the show reached an average of 184,000 weekly viewers across the Dominican Republic. Banco ADOPEM staff have monitored the opening of new savings accounts and deposit making by current account holders by asking if clients have seen the show—43 percent have.

In parallel, Banco ADOPEM initiated a national marketing campaign to encourage women to save. Commercials for the series showcasing the benefits of savings have reached more than 191,000 people on five television networks. Radio advertisements geared toward women have aired on 13 radio stations across the country, using themes and messages similar to the TV commercials. Advertisements are also currently featured on buses in the capital city of Santo Domingo and on billboards in five additional regions outside of the capital city. A critical component of the project is financial education. WWB, in partnership with Reach Global and Puntos de Encuentro, has created a detailed financial education curriculum and trainer's guide that use clips and messages from the television series. WWB and Banco ADOPEM are also working closely with the International Center for Research on Women to conduct an evaluation of the combined impact of the series and the marketing campaign on women's attitudes, perceptions and knowledge, household financial management, financial communication, and savings.

Providing for Health Emergencies

In addition to building savings, women also need a way to protect against health emergencies. Poor women are faced with the daily stress of knowing that a health emergency or unexpected crisis could jeopardize the family's health and living conditions. Research has demonstrated that healthcare costs exert the most financial pressure on poor families as they have little ability to absorb risk. Moreover, medical problems are compounded by the fact that the poor are less likely to seek treatment early in an illness for fear of losing income by taking time away from businesses or other responsibilities. There are also differences in when men and women seek care. In a survey of six sub-Saharan countries, we found that women wait substantially longer (up to nine days) to seek care for themselves versus a child (three days) or spouse (five days). The need to meet the cost of an unexpected health emergency is the most common reason poor families must liquidate their businesses or sell productive assets, such as livestock or equipment. This deprives families of the tools they once had to generate income and further perpetuates the cycle of poverty. The need to provide women with healthcare and the means to pay for it is acute.

To best serve the low-income women, it is essential that product design and delivery take into account women's unique needs. Women face health issues related to pregnancy and childbearing. However, the majority of microinsurance products currently available preclude coverage for many of the most pressing health concerns of women. For example, many health insurance programs exclude pregnancy coverage completely, citing the high costs for insurers and customers. The primary goal should be to create insurance programs that strike a balance between providing coverage that meets the needs of low-income women, while minimizing operating costs for the delivery channels and insurers and keeping premiums low to improve affordability and accessibility. Finding coverage that supports the entire family can be a challenge, often forcing families to pick and choose whom to insure, often leaving women and girls uninsured.

In 2010, WWB helped its network member MFW (Jordan) launch the Caregiver policy (*Ri'aya* in Arabic), a unique micro–health insurance product that provides a cash benefit after hospitalization to help with the costs associated with loss of business, medical expenses, and transportation. Clients can use their coverage on anything from household needs to transportation to a hospital to replacement of lost revenue while their businesses have been closed. Unlike the majority of insurance products available that are typically gender neutral, the Caregiver policy was designed to include coverage of all hospital visits related to pregnancy, a feature that WWB felt was critical to include in order to improve maternal health outcomes. Since the launch of the product, nearly half of claims have been for pregnancy-related health issues. To create the product, WWB and MFW conducted in-depth gender research with more than 1,000 of MFW's clients to gain a thorough understanding of client needs. The study revealed that the majority of MFW's clients were not insured and, when in need of healthcare, used public facilities paid for by savings or borrowings. It was found that most women saw the value of health insurance but viewed cost as a barrier. Since its launch, the product has garnered significant demand from MFW clients with more than 60,000 policies outstanding. Beyond demand, the most important observation concerns the number of claims for pregnancy-related health issues, proving that Jordanian women are using the product not only to protect their businesses but also to protect their own health and well-being.

Expanding Women's Access

Expanding women's access to capital and financial services requires a deep understanding of the needs of women, strong partners willing to make a long-term investment, and belief in the social and economic case for serving women. Financial institutions can provide low-income women and their households with a greater measure of financial security through products and financial education that meet their needs. Women's World Banking partners with its network to increase financial inclusion for millions of people around the globe.

NOTES

[1] Gender baseline studies were conducted in Bosnia and Herzegovina, the Dominican Republic, Jordan, Morocco, Pakistan, and Tunisia. Research related to product development was conducted in Benin, Colombia, Ethiopia, the Gambia, India, Kenya, Mongolia, Peru, Paraguay, and the Philippines.

REFERENCES

Banthia, A., Greene, J., Kawas, C., Lynch, E., and Slama, J. (2011). *Solutions for Financial Inclusion: Serving Rural Women*, New York, NY: Women's World Banking.

Hausmann, R., Tyson L., and Zahidi, S. (2011). *The Global Gender Gap Report 2011*. Geneva, Switzerland: World Economic Forum. Retrieved at http://www3.weforum.org/docs/WEF_GenderGap_Report_2011.pdf

About the Contributors

Penny Abeywardena is the Head of Girls and Women and Associate Director at the Clinton Global Initiative (CGI), a nonpartisan organization that convenes global leaders to devise and implement innovative solutions to the world's most pressing problems. She is responsible for the integration of girls and women–related programming into all of CGI's platforms. Ms. Abeywardena has notably led the growth of girls and women–related commitments; advised multinational corporations, philanthropists, NGOs, and multilateral institutions to increase investments in gender-focused development initiatives; and increased the community of CGI members who are incorporating the gender lens in their work. She is a graduate of the University of Southern California and completed her Masters of International Affairs at Columbia University's School of International and Public Affairs.

Ann Mei Chang is the Senior Advisor for Women and Technology in the Secretary's Office of Global Women's Issues at the U.S. Department of State. Prior to that position, she spent eight years as a Senior Engineering Director at Google in multiple roles, including leading product development for Emerging Markets and leading worldwide engineering for Google's mobile applications and services, where she oversaw 20-fold growth in three years, delivering over $1 billion in annualized revenues. Ms. Chang has served in leadership roles at several other leading Silicon Valley companies including Apple, Macromedia, Intuit, SGI, and some start-ups. She holds a B.S. in Computer Science from Stanford University.

Martha Alter Chen is a Lecturer in Public Policy at the Harvard Kennedy School and International Coordinator of the global research-policy-action network Women in Informal Employment: Globalizing and Organizing (WIEGO). An experienced development practitioner and scholar, Dr. Chen specializes in informal employment, poverty, and gender. Dr. Chen received a PhD in South Asia Regional Studies from the University of Pennsylvania. She is the author or co-author of numerous books, including *The Progress of the World's Women 2005: Women, Work and Poverty*; *Women and Men in the Informal Economy: A Statistical Picture;* and *Perpetual Mourning: Widowhood in Rural India.*

Mary Ellen Iskenderian is President and CEO of Women's World Banking (WWB), the world's largest network of microfinance institutions and banks. Ms. Iskenderian joined WWB in 2006 and leads the WWB global team, based in New York. Prior to WWB, Ms. Iskenderian worked for 17 years at the International Finance Corporation, the private-sector arm of the World Bank. Before that, she worked for the investment bank Lehman Brothers. Ms. Iskenderian serves on the Board of Directors of Kashf Microfinance Bank in Pakistan and is a permanent member of the Council on Foreign Relations. She serves as an Advisor to the Clinton Global Initiative and is a judge for the annual *Financial Times* Sustainable Banking Awards. Ms. Iskenderian holds an MBA from the Yale School of Management and a B.S. in International Economics from Georgetown University's School of Foreign Service.

Beth Kanter writes *Beth's Blog: How Nonprofits Can Use Social Media*, one of the longest running and most popular nonprofit blogs. Her first book, *The Networked Nonprofit*, received Honorable Mention for the Terry McAdams Award. Her second book, *Measuring the Networked Nonprofit*, was published in October 2012. Ms. Kanter has over 30 years' experience working in the nonprofit sector in technology, training, capacity building, evaluation, fundraising, and marketing. *Fast Company* magazine named her as one of the most influential women in technology, and she is included in *Business Week*'s "Voices of Innovation for Social Media." She is a Visiting Scholar, David and Lucile Packard Foundation.

Nüket Kardam is a Professor in the Master of Public Administration Program at Monterey Institute of International Studies (MIIS), a Graduate School of Middlebury College. Prior to joining MIIS, she taught at Pomona College. Dr. Kardam is also a consultant on gender and development, women's leadership, and human rights. She has written on global gender equality norms, on the local applications of women's human rights norms, and on Islam and women's human rights. Her most recent book focuses on Turkey. She holds a PhD in Political Science from Michigan State University.

Jeni Klugman is the Director of Gender and Development at the World Bank Group. Prior to this position, Ms. Klugman was the director and lead author of three global Human Development Reports published by the United Nations Development Programme. From 1992 to 2008, she held various positions at the World Bank, focusing on poverty, inequality, and human development in low-income countries. She currently serves on the World Economic Forum's Advisory Board on Sustainability and Competitiveness and is a fellow of the Human Development and Capabilities Association. Ms. Klugman holds a PhD in Economics from the Australian National University, as well as postgraduate degrees in Law and in Development Economics from Oxford University, where she was a Rhodes Scholar.

Fredric Kropp is a Professor of Entrepreneurship, Creativity and Innovation and Chair of the Fisher International MBA Program at the Monterey Institute of International Studies, in California. He also holds an adjunct professor position in the Entrepreneurship, Commercialisation and Innovation Centre at The University of Adelaide, in Australia. His teaching and research focuses on entrepreneurship and social entrepreneurship, in particular, what motivates entrepreneurs and makes them successful. Prior to academia, Dr. Kropp was an economist and consultant focused on policy analysis, market planning, and forecasting for Fortune 500 and government clients. He still works with start-up ventures and nonprofit organizations.

Arwa Othman is a civic activist and writer, based in Sana'a, Yemen, where she focuses on heritage and anthropology at the Yemen Centre for Studies and Research. In 2004, Ms. Othman founded *Bayt Al-maouroth* (Folkloric Heritage House), which houses a museum, a research center, and a gallery that preserve and celebrate Yemini folklore. Ms. Othman is an award-winning journalist contributing to several Yemeni newspapers. In 2001, she received the Arab Creativity Award at the Sharjah International Literary Festival. Ms. Othman also received, from the Il Club delle Donna Association, the 28th International Minerva Anna Maria Mammoliti prize in 2011 for her cultural activism and defense of women's rights. She participated actively in Change Square during the youth revolution in Yemen.

Trish Tierney is Executive Director of the Institute of International Education in San Francisco, where she founded the Institute's Center for Women's Leadership Initiatives and manages a diverse portfolio of global leadership, education, and exchange programs in partnership with the U.S. Department of State, women-led NGOs, and private sector partners. Ms. Tierney has led the growth of IIE's women-focused programs, especially in science, technology, engineering, and math. Ms. Tierney began her international education career as a volunteer teacher in Namibia, followed by positions at the World Bank and Cisco Systems. She holds a B.A. from the University of Notre Dame, and an M.A. from the Johns Hopkins School of Advanced International Studies.

Sarah Twigg is a consultant in the World Bank's Gender and Development Unit. In her current role she conducts research on a range of areas related to gender equality issues and supports communications, outreach, and advocacy efforts in support of the World Bank's gender and development priorities. Prior to joining the World Bank, she worked as a researcher for two global Human Development Reports published by the United Nations Development Programme and as a gender and climate finance consultant for UN Women. Ms. Twigg also has more than five years' experience practicing as a lawyer in New Zealand and New York.

Melanne Verveer is the former U.S. Ambassador-at-Large for Global Women's Issues. In that role, she mobilized concrete support for women's empowerment through initiatives and programs designed to increase women's and girls' access to education and healthcare, to combat violence against women and girls, and to ensure that women's rights were fully integrated with human rights in the development of U.S. foreign policy. Her previous roles include serving as Chair and Co-CEO of Vital Voices Global Partnership, an international nonprofit she co-founded, and serving as Assistant to the President and Chief of Staff to the First Lady in the Clinton Administration. Ms. Verveer has a B.A. and M.A. from Georgetown University. She is currently the Executive Director of the Georgetown Institute for Women, Peace and Security.

IIE's Center for Women's Leadership Initiatives

The IIE Center for Women's Leadership Initiatives (WLI) provides opportunities for women worldwide to participate in cutting-edge training, professional development and exchange programs and pursue higher education. Through our programs, women develop and join networks of peers, mentors and experts and serve as effective leaders in the public and private sectors around the world.

Our innovative partnership approach supports women to become leaders in their communities, fields and sectors. We work with sponsors to design programs that leverage strategic partnerships to engage emerging and established women leaders from underserved communities. Our programs create linkages among individuals, groups and networks, resulting in a tangible multiplier effect, measurable impact and long-term sustainability.

Learn: Building knowledge and skills among organizations and the women they serve.

- *Training and Education. In partnership with nonprofit, education, business and government sectors, WLI programs provide short-term training, workshops, mentorships and higher education opportunities for women.*
- *Curricula. IIE develops customized curricula for targeted audiences from underserved women to emerging and established women leaders.*
- *Leadership. Our community grants programs empower leaders to use their new-found skills and knowledge to extend their work and make a lasting impact on local communities.*
- *Capacity. Our programs build the capacity of local organizations, experts, leaders and trainers leading to sustainable and locally driven, long-term impact.*

Connect: Linking women with resources and networks.

- *Networks. We provide technical assistance and resources to build locally-driven sustainable networks through which women can mobilize around issues of mutual interest and engage in activities to advance their goals.*

- *Public-Private Partnerships. We leverage partnerships with leading companies, governments and NGOs to support and engage women in mentoring, training and networking opportunities.*
- *Local Engagement. We partner with local NGOs and community organizations to implement programs effectively and build local capacity.*
- *Exchange Programs. IIE administers many of the world's most dynamic and prestigious scholarship and exchange programs, many with an emphasis on developing and advancing women leaders.*

Achieve: Promoting women as leading innovators and change makers.

- *Women trained through Women in Technology (WIT) started more than 60 new businesses in the Middle East and North Africa. WIT provided more than 2,500 low income women with scholarships. WIT was sponsored by the U.S. Department of State's Middle East Partnership Initiative (MEPI), with support from Microsoft and Cisco Systems.*
- *Women make up over 30 percent of all rescued scholars in South and Central Asia and over 20 percent of those rescued in the Middle East through IIE's Scholar Rescue Fund.*
- *Nearly 150 women from the Bay Area have served as Professional and Cultural mentors to 78 TechWomen Emerging Leaders from the Middle East and North Africa over the last two years. Past TechWomen participants have launched and grown businesses and have started critical initiatives in their home countries. The 2013 program expanded to include new countries in North and Sub-Saharan Africa and will involve double the number of participants.*

Key initiatives include:

African Centers of Excellence for Women's Leadership (ACE –Leaders)

ACE-Leaders is designed to support four organizations in Kenya, Rwanda, Uganda and Ethiopia to become centers of excellence in women's advocacy and leadership training in Sub-Saharan Africa. These groups work in three critical development areas: economic empowerment, family planning and girls' education. ACE-Leaders is sponsored by the David and Lucille Packard Foundation.

Higher Education Readiness Program (HER)

In spring 2013, IIE will launch a major new initiative to provide young women from underserved communities with pathways to university: The IIE Higher Education Readiness Program (HER), a new three-year pilot project in Ethiopia, will provide 100 girls entering the 11th grade with scholarship support combined with innovative leadership and life skills training to help them complete their secondary education and equip them with the tools needed to continue on to university. The IIE HER Program will be launched with seed funding from the Institute. IIE is actively seeking funding partners for this new initiative.

TechWomen

An initiative of the U.S. Department of State, Bureau of Educational and Cultural Affairs, TechWomen brings emerging women leaders and entrepreneurs from the Middle East and Africa to the United States for a professional mentorship and cultural exchange program, where they are paired with their counterparts in San Francisco and Silicon Valley. TechWomen fosters and develops the next generation of women leaders in the fields of Science, Technology, Engineering and Math (STEM) by providing women and girls with the access and opportunity needed to pursue careers in STEM.

WES

Women's Enterprise for Sustainability (WES) empowers women-led organizations in Tunisia to operate training centers as social enterprises offering courses in leadership, entrepreneurship and social media. Through these centers, aspiring and established women entrepreneurs across Tunisia gain new skills and networks, launch new businesses, and develop as innovative leaders in their communities. WES is sponsored by the U.S. Department of State's Middle East Partnership Initiative (MEPI).

IIE Information and Resources

THE CENTER FOR INTERNATIONAL PARTNERSHIPS IN HIGHER EDUCATION

The IIE Center for International Partnerships in Higher Education draws on IIE's wide-ranging network of more than 1,100 colleges and universities and extensive expertise in international education to provide administrators, policymakers, and practitioners with the resources and connections to develop and sustain partnerships around the world. Major initiatives of the Center are the International Academic Partnerships Program and the IIE Global Partner Service. The Center also produces timely policy research and convenes international education leaders in conferences and workshops.

WEBSITE: www.iie.org/cip

THE CENTER FOR ACADEMIC MOBILITY RESEARCH

The IIE Center for Academic Mobility Research brings together the Institute's in-house research expertise with leading minds from around the world to conduct and disseminate timely and relevant research and policy analysis in the field of international student and faculty mobility. The Center provides applied research and program evaluation services to domestic and international governmental agencies, nongovernmental organizations, corporations, and foundations. The Center's in-depth books and reports, including the well-known *Open Doors Report on International Educational Exchange*, supported by the U.S. Department of State, are key reference resources. In addition, the Center's policy papers and snapshot surveys capture trends in the changing landscape of international education.

WEBSITE: www.iie.org/mobility

RECENT IIE WHITE AND BRIEFING PAPERS

IIE Papers address the changing landscape of international education, offering timely snapshots of critical issues in the field.

- U.S. Students in China: Meeting the Goals of the 100,000 Strong Initiative (2013)
- Expanding U.S. Study Abroad to Brazil: A Guide for Institutions (2012)
- Models for U.S. Study Abroad to Indonesia (2012)
- U.S. and Australian International Student Data Collection: Key Differences and Practices (2012)
- Learn by Doing: Expanding International Internships/Work Abroad Opportunities for U.S. STEM Students (2012)
- English-Taught Master's Programs in Europe: New Findings on Supply and Demand (2012)
- U.S. Students in Overseas Degree Programs: Key Destinations and Fields of Study (2012)

- Joint and Double Degree Programs in a Global Context (September 2011)
- Expanding U.S. Study Abroad to India: A Guide for Institutions (July 2011)
- Evaluating and Measuring the Impact of Citizen Diplomacy: Current State and Future Directions (July 2011)
- Building Sustainable U.S.-Ethiopian University Partnerships: Findings from a Conference (July 2011)

WEBSITE: www.iie.org/publications

IIE/AIFS FOUNDATION GLOBAL EDUCATION RESEARCH REPORTS

This series of books explores the most pressing and underresearched issues affecting international education policy today.

- *Women in the Global Economy: Leading Social Change*
- *Latin America's New Knowledge Economy: Higher Education, Government, and International Collaboration* (February 2013)
- *Developing Strategic International Partnerships: Models for Initiating and Sustaining Innovative Institutional Linkages* (October 2011)
- *Who Goes Where and Why? An Overview and Analysis of Global Educational Mobility* (April 2011)
- *Innovation through Education: Building the Knowledge Economy in the Middle East* (August 2010)
- *International India: A Turning Point in Educational Exchange with the U.S.* (January 2010)
- *Higher Education on the Move: New Developments in Global Mobility* (April 2009)
- *U.S.-China Educational Exchange: Perspectives on a Growing Partnership* (October 2008)

WEBSITE: www.iie.org/gerr

IIE Web Resources

IIEPASSPORT.ORG

This free online search engine lists nearly 10,000 study abroad programs worldwide and provides advisers with hands-on tools to counsel students and promote study abroad.

WEBSITE: www.iiepassport.org

STUDY ABROAD FUNDING

This valuable funding resource helps U.S. students find funding for study abroad programs.

WEBSITE: www.studyabroadfunding.org

FUNDING FOR UNITED STATES STUDY

This directory offers the most relevant data on hundreds of fellowships, grants, paid internships, and scholarships for study in the United States.

WEBSITE: www.fundingusstudy.org

INTENSIVE ENGLISH USA

Comprehensive reference with more than 500 accredited English language programs in the United States.

WEBSITE: www.intensiveenglishusa.org

FULBRIGHT PROGRAMS FOR U.S. STUDENTS

The Fulbright U.S. Student Program equips future American leaders with the skills they need to thrive in an increasingly global environment by providing funding for one academic year of study or research abroad, to be conducted after graduation from an accredited university.

SPONSOR: U.S. Department of State, Bureau of Educational and Cultural Affairs

WEBSITE: http://us.fulbrightonline.org

FULBRIGHT PROGRAMS FOR U.S. SCHOLARS

The traditional Fulbright Scholar Program sends hundreds of U.S. faculty and professionals abroad each year. Grantees lecture and conduct research in a wide variety of academic and professional fields.

SPONSOR: U.S. Department of State, Bureau of Educational and Cultural Affairs

WEBSITE: www.cies.org

Programs of the AIFS Foundation

The AIFS Foundation

The mission of the AIFS Foundation is to provide educational and cultural exchange opportunities to foster greater understanding among the people of the world. It seeks to fulfill this mission by organizing high-quality educational opportunities for students and providing grants to individuals and schools for participation in culturally enriching educational programs.

WEBSITE: www.aifsfoundation.org

ACADEMIC YEAR IN AMERICA (AYA)

Each year, AYA brings nearly 1,000 high school students from around the world to the United States. They come for the school year to live with American families and attend local high schools, learning about American culture and sharing their own languages and customs with their host families.

WEBSITE: www.academicyear.org

FUTURE LEADERS EXCHANGE PROGRAM (FLEX)

Established in 1992 under the FREEDOM Support Act and administered by the U.S. Department of State's Bureau of Educational and Cultural Affairs, FLEX encourages long-lasting peace and mutual understanding between the United States and the countries of Eurasia.

YOUTH EXCHANGE AND STUDY PROGRAM (YES)

Since 2002, this U.S. Department of State high school exchange program has enabled students from predominantly Muslim countries to learn about American society and values, acquire leadership skills, and help educate Americans about their countries and cultures.

Programs of the American Institute for Foreign Study

American Institute For Foreign Study

The AIFS mission is to enrich the lives of young people throughout the world by providing them with educational and cultural exchange programs of the highest possible quality.

WEBSITE: www.aifs.com

AIFS COLLEGE STUDY ABROAD

AIFS is a leading provider of study abroad programs for college students. Students can study abroad for a summer, semester, or academic year in 17 countries around the world. Faculty-led and customized programs are also offered.

WEBSITE: www.aifsabroad.com

AMERICAN COUNCIL FOR INTERNATIONAL STUDIES (ACIS)

For more than 30 years, ACIS has helped students and their teachers discover the world through premier travel and education. Teachers can choose destinations throughout Europe, the Americas, and Asia.

WEBSITE: www.acis.com

AU PAIR IN AMERICA

Au Pair in America makes it possible for nearly 4,000 eager and skilled young adults from around the world to join American families and help care for their children during a mutually rewarding, yearlong cultural exchange experience.

WEBSITE: www.aupairinamerica.com

CAMP AMERICA

Each summer, Camp America brings nearly 6,000 young people from around the world to the United States to work as camp counselors and camp staff.

WEBSITE: www.campamerica.aifs.com

CULTURAL INSURANCE SERVICES INTERNATIONAL (CISI)

CISI is the leading provider of study abroad and international student insurance coverage. Since 1992, CISI has insured more than 1 million international students and cultural exchange participants worldwide.

WEBSITE: www.culturalinsurance.com

SUMMER INSTITUTE FOR THE GIFTED (SIG)

SIG is a three-week academic, recreational, and social summer program for gifted and talented students. Students from around the world in grades 4 through 11 can participate in SIG Residential programs offered at university campuses across the country including Columbia University, Princeton University, Yale University, UC Berkeley, UCLA, Amherst College, Emory University, Bryn Mawr College, Vassar College, and University of Texas at Austin. Day, part-time and Saturday programs are also offered, as well as University Prep programs at selected institutions. SIG operates under the National Society for the Gifted and the Talented (NSGT), which is a nonprofit 501(c)3 organization.

WEBSITE: www.giftedstudy.org

AIFS Information and Resources

The following resources are available for download at www.aifsabroad.com/advisors/publications.asp

- Student Guide to Study Abroad and Career Development
- Diversity in International Education Summary Report
- The Gender Gap in Post-Secondary Study Abroad: Understanding and Marketing to Male Students
- Study Abroad: A 21st Century Perspective, Vol I
- Study Abroad: A 21st Century Perspective, Vol II: The Changing Landscape
- Innocents at Home Redux—The Continuing Challenge to America's Future
- Impact on Education Abroad on Career Development, Vol. I
- Impact on Education Abroad on Career Development: Four Community College Case Studies, Vol. II